The Art of Moving On

Healing after heartbreak

The Art of Moving On

Healing after heartbreak

ANURAG PAUL

AMARYLLIS

AMARYLLIS

An imprint of Manjul Publishing House Pvt. Ltd.
• C-16, Sector 3, Noida, Uttar Pradesh 201 301, India
Website: www.manjulindia.com
Registered Office:
• 2nd Floor, Usha Preet Complex, 42 Malviya Nagar,
Bhopal 462 003 – India
Distribution Centres
Ahmedabad, Bengaluru, Chennai, Hyderabad,
Kochi, Kolkata, Mumbai, Noida, Pune

The Art of Moving On: Healing after heartbreak by Anurag Paul

This edition published in paperback by
Amaryllis, an imprint of Manjul Publishing House in 2025

ISBN 978-93-5543-860-7

Printed and bound in India by Thomson Press (India) Ltd.

Contents

DEDICATION

To you, the courageous reader, gently gather the broken pieces of your heart and believe that something brighter awaits despite the pain. This book is for the moments you've felt lost, the tears you've silently shed, and the hope you've clung to even when it seemed distant. May these pages whisper encouragement, reminding you that within your heart lies the power to heal, grow, and rediscover love in ways you never thought possible.

Introduction

Heartbreak can be one of the most isolating and painful experiences we encounter. It often leaves us feeling unmoored, questioning our worth, and wondering if life will ever feel whole again. Yet, in the depths of this despair lies a powerful opportunity for transformation. When we allow ourselves to acknowledge and work through heartbreak, we don't just move on— we emerge stronger, wiser, and more authentically ourselves.

The Art of Moving On is designed to guide you through every phase of healing, from the initial shock of loss to the empowered steps you take towards a brighter future. This book is divided into five parts, each focusing on a distinct stage of your emotional recovery and growth. By understanding what's happening inside your heart and mind, you'll discover practical tools, compassionate insights, and real-world examples that will encourage you to move forward with renewed hope and confidence.

Part I: Understanding the Roots of Heartbreak

This foundational section explores why heartbreak hurts so deeply and how it has been perceived across different eras and cultures. You'll learn to:

- Recognise the true nature of heartbreak by looking at its emotional, physiological, and historical aspects.
- Define heartbreak beyond "just sadness," examining how grief, denial, and longing all intertwine.
- Trace heartbreak's timeline and see how these phases mirror the grieving process.
- Reflect on the lessons that centuries of human experience have provided, reassuring you that heartbreak is a universal—and surmountable—experience.

By the end of Part I, you will understand that your pain has a purpose. Realising the roots of heartbreak helps you see it not merely as an end, but as a pivotal turning point in your story.

Part II: Transforming Pain into Power

Once you grasp the deeper layers of heartbreak, it's time to harness your pain and begin your healing journey.

This section focuses on:

- Turning pain into a catalyst for change, allowing you to reclaim strength instead of sinking into despair.
- Learning practical techniques for letting go of what you cannot change, and creating space—both physically and emotionally—for new perspectives.
- Exploring inspiring, real-life stories of individuals who have successfully navigated the hardest parts of heartbreak, reminding you that you are not alone.

Part II offers hope and shows you that, with patience and effort, you can transform the darkest moments of life into powerful agents for growth and renewal.

Part III: Embracing Acceptance and Renewal

Here, we delve deeper into the delicate process of accepting what's happened and shifting your outlook:

- Embrace your emotional mosaic by recognising that heartbreak involves a range of feelings—anger, grief, yearning, and eventually acceptance.
- Learn why acceptance is a true gateway to transformation rather than a sign of giving up.
- Discover how letting go of resistance and surrendering to the present can profoundly alter your path towards healing.

In Part III, you'll find that acceptance brings a sense of peace and opens the door to genuine renewal—a space where past wounds no longer define you.

Part IV: Reconnecting with Your Inner Self

Once you've reached a level of acceptance, it's time to rediscover the incredible individual you are and rekindle your sense of purpose:

- Identify your core values and use them as a guiding light to regain confidence and self-belief.
- Reawaken your passions by exploring the interests that once ignited excitement within you, and by nurturing new avenues of curiosity.
- Cultivate solitude and self-compassion as pathways to true self-discovery, understanding that spending quality time with yourself is crucial for healing.
- Craft a personal manifesto that captures who you are becoming and the future you wish to create.

By focusing on these insights, Part IV helps you rebuild your identity so you can step forward with authenticity, joy, and a clear sense of direction.

Part V: Stepping into a Renewed Future

Finally, having laid the groundwork for healing, acceptance, and self-discovery, you are ready to chart a path towards a vibrant new phase of life:

- Define the milestones and meaningful goals that will keep you motivated and celebrating progress along the way.
- Redefine success to align with your values, aspirations, and hard-won insights.
- Discover how to rise from the ashes stronger than before, armed with resilience and a roadmap to maintain balance between stability and necessary change.
- Embrace the courage that has always resided within, taking bold steps towards a life that honours both your past lessons and your bright possibilities ahead.

Part V solidifies your transformation, reminding you that although heartbreak once weighed you down, you now possess the strength, clarity, and passion to face new beginnings with unwavering conviction.

This book was written to remind you of your capacity to heal and rebuild—a process that requires understanding, patience, and courage. Alongside practical steps and inspirational stories, you'll discover that each broken piece of your heart can become a stepping stone to a future brimming with opportunities for love, fulfillment, and self-discovery.

No matter where you stand today, know that heartbreak doesn't define you. Together, we'll walk through these pages, unveiling the art of moving on—an art that begins and ends with embracing your inherent resilience and unwavering ability to grow. The chapters ahead offer you wisdom, strategies, and hope to transform heartbreak into a powerful catalyst for the life you deserve. Welcome to your journey of renewal.

ACKNOWLEDGEMENTS

I am deeply grateful to those who have supported me throughout this journey.

To my parents, thank you for instilling a love for words and storytelling in me. Your unwavering encouragement has made this book possible.

To my brother, Akash, your insights and strength have been invaluable, and I feel fortunate to have you by my side.

To my wife Jyoti, my muse and greatest champion, I couldn't have done this without your steadfast belief in me.

Finally, heartfelt thanks to every reader and the supportive community that has cheered me on. Your encouragement has been a guiding light, and I hope this book offers solace, inspiration, and the reassurance that brighter days are always within reach.

Part I

Understanding the Roots of Heartbreak

Chapter 1

The Anatomy of Heartbreak

Heartbreak is one of the most profound human experiences. It touches everyone at some point, transcending age, culture, and background. Yet, its impact is often underestimated—dismissed as something we should "just get over." But anyone who has lived through the searing pain of a broken heart knows it isn't that simple. Heartbreak feels like an all-consuming storm, leaving us raw and vulnerable. Why does it hurt so much? The answer lies in how heartbreak affects both our minds and bodies.

When we lose someone, we deeply care about, our brains and bodies undergo a dramatic shift. From a neurological standpoint, heartbreak triggers the same areas of the brain associated with physical pain. This is why it doesn't just feel emotional—it's also physical.

The ache in your chest, the knots in your stomach, and the heaviness in your limbs are all tangible symptoms.

Even more striking is how heartbreak mimics withdrawal from addiction. When you're in love, your brain is flooded with dopamine, the "feel-good" neurotransmitter, creating a euphoria. This is why being with someone you love feels like a high. But when the relationship ends, those dopamine levels plummet, and your brain struggles to cope with the sudden absence of its "reward." This withdrawal process explains the longing, cravings, and obsessive thoughts that often accompany heartbreak.

One of the most challenging aspects of heartbreak is the mind's tendency to fixate on the lost relationship. Memories replay like a broken record—conversations, shared moments, and even imagined reconciliation scenarios flood your thoughts. Neuroscience calls this rumination, and while it may feel like you're losing control, it's simply your brain's way of trying to make sense of the loss.

Imagine a child searching for a misplaced toy, believing its return will restore their happiness. Similarly, your brain keeps returning to the relationship, convinced that understanding or resolving it will end the pain. But this fixation can trap you in a cycle of grief, making it feel like the storm will never pass.

Heartbreak also triggers a cascade of emotions, often referred to as the stages of grief. These emotions are not linear—they ebb and flow, often overlapping unpredictably. Recognising them can help you navigate the storm:

1. **Denial:** In the initial phase, the loss feels unreal. You might replay conversations or recheck messages, hoping for a sign that the breakup isn't permanent. This is your mind's way of cushioning the blow.
2. **Anger:** As reality sets in, anger often follows. You might direct it at your ex, yourself, or even the world. While uncomfortable, anger is a sign that you're processing the loss.
3. **Bargaining:** You may fantasise about "what ifs." What if you had done things differently? What if they change their mind? Bargaining is a desperate attempt to regain control over the uncontrollable.
4. **Grief:** Grief is the most profound stage, marked by sadness, regret, and emptiness.

It's a natural response to losing someone who meant so much to you. Each stage is part of the healing process, not a reflection of weakness.

So, how can understanding these responses help you move forward? Awareness is the first step. When you know why your brain and body are reacting this way, you can approach your pain with compassion instead of frustration.

Here are practical steps to harness this understanding for growth:

1. **Accept Your Feelings Without Judgment**

   Allow yourself to feel the pain without labelling it as "bad" or "wrong." Acknowledge, "I'm feeling this way because I cared deeply." Accepting your emotions creates space for healing.

2. **Disrupt the Rumination Cycle**

   Instead of fighting your thoughts, redirect them. Create a list of activities that require focus—like solving a puzzle, cooking a new recipe, or taking a yoga class. These activities engage your brain in the present, reducing its hold on the past.

3. **Practice Mindful Detachment**

   Mindfulness doesn't mean forgetting your ex; it means observing your thoughts without clinging to them. Try this: when a memory surfaces, acknowledge it with a phrase like, "This is just a thought," and then gently return your focus to the present.

4. **Reframe the Narrative**

   Heartbreak isn't just an ending—it's a turning point. Reflect on what you've learned about yourself, your values, and your needs. Journaling can be a powerful tool to uncover insights and track your progress.

5. **Seek Connection, Not Isolation**

   While solitude can help you process your emotions, don't isolate yourself. Spend time with supportive friends or join a community that resonates with your interests. Connection reminds you that you're not alone.

Understanding heartbreak is like finding a flashlight in a dark storm. It doesn't stop the rain, but it gives you the clarity to navigate your way through. As painful as it feels, this storm is also a chance to grow—to rediscover your strength, redefine your identity, and rebuild your life.

The journey ahead won't be easy, but you've already taken the first step by seeking understanding. And with every small step forward, you'll find that the storm begins to clear, and a new horizon awaits.

Chapter 2

Defining Heartbreak: More Than Just Sadness

Heartbreak is often dismissed as mere sadness, a passing phase we're expected to overcome quickly. But at its core, heartbreak is far more complex. It's an intense emotional experience that transcends simple definitions, encompassing grief, longing, and a sense of emotional disorientation. To truly understand it, we must explore its layers, origins, and role in shaping our human experience.

Heartbreak is the emotional aftermath of loss, often triggered by the end of a romantic relationship but not limited to it. It involves:

1. **Grief:** The deep sadness stemming from losing something or someone cherished.

Unlike other forms of sadness, grief often feels like an empty space in your life—a void that nothing seems able to fill.

2. **Longing:** A persistent yearning for what once was. This longing can manifest in a desire to return to the relationship or a fixation on memories that seem brighter in hindsight.
3. **Emotional Disorientation:** Losing a relationship can disrupt your sense of identity and stability. It's not just about losing the person—it's about losing the future you envisioned with them, leaving you unsure of your path forward.

Heartbreak isn't simply one emotion: it's a whirlwind of many, sometimes conflicting, feelings. Recognising this complexity helps us approach it with greater understanding and compassion.

The term "heartbreak" has deep linguistic and cultural roots. Its etymology traces back to Old English and Middle French, meaning "a breaking of the heart." This metaphorical language reflects how the experience feels—a deep, splitting pain in the center of our emotional being.

Across cultures, heartbreak has been recognised as a profound human experience. In ancient Greek philosophy, heartbreak was seen as a disruption of the soul's harmony. In Japanese culture, the term koi no yokan captures the idea of love that feels inevitable and, by extension, the heartbreak that often follows when that connection is severed. This universal acknowledgment of heartbreak underscores its ubiquity in human life.

Heartbreak exists at the intersection of loss and love, making it one of the most profound emotions we can experience. Its intensity often feels disproportionate because it doesn't just represent the end of a relationship; it forces us to confront deeper questions: Who am I without this person? What does this loss say about me?

This introspection is both painful and transformative. While heartbreak can feel like the collapse of your world, it also creates a unique opportunity to re-evaluate your values, desires, and goals. In this way, heartbreak can catalyse personal growth, pushing you to rebuild stronger and wiser.

One of the most common misconceptions about heartbreak is that it's simply sadness. While sadness is a component, heartbreak also includes confusion, anger, regret, and even moments of relief. Reducing it to sadness minimises its complexity and discourages the deep processing required for healing.

Another misconception is that heartbreak is a sign of weakness. On the contrary, heartbreak is a testament to your capacity to love deeply and vulnerably. It's an experience that unites us all in our shared humanity.

Understanding heartbreak in depth allows us to approach it as more than a temporary affliction. Instead, we can see it as an integral part of the human emotional spectrum, which shapes us profoundly.

Here are practical ways to embrace this understanding:

1. **Reframe Heartbreak as Growth**

   View it as a turning point rather than seeing heartbreak as an end. Consider journaling about what this experience teaches you—about yourself, your needs, and your values.

2. **Acknowledge Its Multifaceted Nature**

   Make a list of the emotions you're feeling. By naming them, you begin to demystify the experience and permit yourself to feel everything without judgment.

3. **Seek a Cultural or Historical Perspective**

   Explore how heartbreak has been expressed in art, literature, or music from different cultures. This reminds you of its universality and inspires you to find your way to process and express your pain.

4. **Embrace the Introspection**

   Ask yourself more profound questions: What did this relationship mean to me? How has it shaped who I am? This isn't about dwelling on the past but learning from it to build a better future.

By understanding heartbreak's true nature, we can appreciate its role in our lives—not as something to avoid or suppress but as an experience that deepens our capacity for love and resilience. In the chapters ahead, we'll continue this journey, delving into how heartbreak challenges us, reshapes us, and ultimately transforms us.

You're not just surviving heartbreak but navigating one of life's most profound emotional experiences. And with each step, you're becoming stronger, wiser, and more attuned to the person you're meant to be.

Chapter 3

Lessons From the Timeline of Heartbreak

Heartbreak is often described as a personal journey, yet its milestones echo a universal experience. By tracing the emotional timeline—from shock to acceptance—we find pain and opportunities for healing and growth. Each stage contributes uniquely to mending a broken heart, offering lessons about resilience, self-discovery, and renewal.

In this chapter, we will examine how these emotional phases shape our recovery and what they teach us about ourselves. Additionally, we'll explore how humanity's collective wisdom about heartbreak can guide us through even the darkest moments.

The initial shock of heartbreak feels like the

ground being ripped from under you. It's disorienting, leaving you scrambling for stability. But as painful as it is, this shattering moment serves a hidden purpose: it forces you to be present with your emotions.

Heartbreak compels us to feel deeply in a world where we often suppress discomfort. It reminds us that pain is a natural response to loss—a testament to the depth of our love and connection. Accepting this reality, rather than resisting it, lays the foundation for healing.

Lesson: Embrace the pain as part of your humanity. Allow yourself to sit with your feelings, even when they're uncomfortable. This isn't about dwelling on the hurt but acknowledging it as a necessary step toward wholeness.

Denial is often misunderstood as avoidance, but it's better seen as your brain's way of protecting you from emotional overload. It allows you to process the breakup gradually, giving you time to adjust to a new reality.

However, staying in denial for too long can hinder progress. Recognising when it's time to move forward is key. This phase teaches us the importance of balancing emotional safety with the courage to face the truth.

Lesson: Use denial as a temporary refuge, not a permanent home. When you're ready, take small steps to confront the reality of your loss, whether through honest conversations with a trusted friend or journaling your thoughts.

Anger often emerges as a fiery response to the injustice of heartbreak. It might be directed at your ex, the circumstances, or even yourself. While anger can feel overwhelming, it holds a vital purpose: it helps you reclaim a sense of control.

In this phase, you're no longer passive in your pain. Anger energises you to act by setting boundaries, seeking clarity, or pursuing personal goals. When channeled constructively, it becomes a force for transformation.

Lesson: Recognise anger as a sign of progress, but don't let it consume you. Channel it into positive actions, such as creating new habits, asserting your needs, or pursuing a passion you've put on hold.

Depression is often the quietest yet heaviest phase of heartbreak. In this stage, the full weight of the loss settles in, bringing feelings of sadness, regret, and isolation. But within this stillness lies an opportunity for profound reflection.

You're left with yourself when the noise of denial and anger subsides. This is a time to ask deeper questions: What does this loss teach me about my needs and boundaries? What do I truly value in a relationship? By leaning into these questions, you begin to uncover insights that pave the way for growth.

Lesson: Allow yourself to grieve, but also use

this phase to rediscover your inner strength. Seek out activities that nourish your soul, such as meditation, creative expression, or spending time in nature.

Acceptance is the final stage, but it's not about forgetting or erasing the past. Instead, it's about making peace with what happened and integrating the experience into your story. In this phase, you begin to see the breakup not as a defining loss but as a stepping stone to a brighter future.

Acceptance teaches us resilience—the ability to move forward while carrying the lessons of the past. It's a reminder that we are not defined by what happens to us, but by how we choose to respond.

Lesson: Celebrate your progress, no matter how small. Reflect on how far you've come and what you've learned about yourself. Use these insights to set intentions for the future, focusing on growth and self-empowerment.

Throughout history, heartbreak has been a wellspring of wisdom and creativity. The experience has inspired countless works of art, literature, and music, from Shakespeare's sonnets to modern-day breakup songs. This shared expression reminds us that we're not alone in our pain.

In ancient cultures, heartbreak was often seen as a rite of passage—a crucible for personal transformation. The Japanese concept of wabi-sabi, which celebrates imperfection and transience, encourages us to find beauty in life's broken pieces. Similarly, Native

American traditions speak of the heart as a place of deep wisdom, suggesting that even pain can bring clarity.

Lesson: Draw strength from the universality of heartbreak. Read a poem, listen to a song, or explore a cultural tradition that resonates with your experience. Let it remind you that you are part of a larger story of resilience and renewal.

By mapping the emotional timeline of heartbreak, we uncover pain and purpose. Each stage—shock, denial, anger, depression, and acceptance—contributes to our healing in unique ways. Together, they create a journey of transformation, teaching us about love, loss, and the resilience of the human spirit.

Heartbreak doesn't have to define you. It can refine you, shaping a stronger, wiser, and more compassionate version of yourself. The road ahead may be challenging, but it is also filled with opportunities for growth and renewal. Let this knowledge guide you as you move forward, one step at a time.

Chapter 4

Heartbreak Through the Ages

Heartbreak is not just a personal experience—it's a thread woven through the fabric of human history. Across centuries, it has inspired some of the most profound art, literature, and cultural traditions. By exploring how heartbreak has been depicted and understood in different eras, we uncover the shared nature of this experience and its role in shaping creativity and resilience.

In ancient mythology, heartbreak wasn't limited to mortals; even gods and heroes faced the anguish of love lost. The Greek myth of Orpheus and Eurydice tells of Orpheus descending into the underworld to bring back his beloved, only to lose her forever due to a moment of doubt. This story reflects the timeless struggle to hold onto love, even when it seems impossible.

Similarly, the story of Isis and Osiris in Egyptian mythology portrays heartbreak as a source of strength. When Osiris is killed and dismembered, Isis's devotion drives her to search for his body parts and resurrect him, symbolizing the lengths we go to for love and healing.

Lesson: Ancient myths teach us that heartbreak, though painful, is a testament to the depth of our love and the strength of our commitment. Even in loss, there is room for courage and transformation.

In ancient Rome, love and heartbreak were often viewed pragmatically. Stoicism, a philosophy popular in Roman culture, encouraged individuals to face loss with calm acceptance. Roman poets like Ovid, however, revealed the raw emotions beneath this stoic exterior. His *Amores* and *Ars Amatoria* explore the joys and sorrows of love, offering insights into the vulnerability that even the most disciplined hearts experience.

For the Romans, heartbreak was a test of character—a chance to prove resilience and maintain dignity in the face of emotional upheaval.

Lesson: The Roman perspective reminds us that while heartbreak is inevitable, how we respond to it defines us. Accepting pain as part of life allows us to move forward with grace and strength.

The Middle Ages brought the concept of courtly love, where longing and heartbreak were almost romanticised. Troubadours sang of unrequited love, and knights undertook great quests to win the favour of unattainable ladies. Stories like *Tristan and Isolde* elevated love's pain to a noble pursuit, portraying heartbreak as both a source of suffering and inspiration.

This era framed heartbreak as an integral part of the human condition, a force that could lead to personal growth or spiritual enlightenment. It also reflected societal norms where duty and social expectations often constrained love.

Lesson: The medieval portrayal of heartbreak shows us that even in suffering, there is beauty and meaning. Pain can fuel creativity and push us to seek higher understanding.

The Victorian era celebrated intense emotional expression, and heartbreak was often depicted as a life-altering event. Romantic literature, such as Charlotte Brontë's *Jane Eyre* or Emily Brontë's *Wuthering Heights,* explored themes of unrequited love, betrayal, and the enduring power of passion. These works emphasised the transformative nature of heartbreak, showing characters who emerged stronger or tragically broken.

Victorian attitudes toward heartbreak also highlighted the tension between societal expectations and personal desires. Love was seen as both a sacred bond and a source of inner turmoil, reflecting the complexity of human relationships.

Lesson: Victorian narratives remind us that

heartbreak, while deeply emotional, can lead to profound self-discovery. It encourages us to honour our emotions while seeking personal growth.

In contemporary times, heartbreak has evolved from being a private pain to a public conversation. Music, film, and social media have become platforms for expressing and processing heartbreak. Songs like Adele's "Someone Like You" or films like *Eternal Sunshine of the Spotless Mind* resonate with audiences because they capture the universal nature of loss and longing.

Modern portrayals of heartbreak emphasise empowerment and resilience. Where older narratives often focus on enduring pain, today's stories encourage moving forward, setting boundaries, and prioritising self-care. This shift reflects a cultural embrace of emotional authenticity and mental health awareness.

Lesson: Modern perspectives on heartbreak encourage us to view it not just as an end but as a beginning. It's an opportunity to prioritise self-love and redefine our future on our terms.

Through the ages, heartbreak has been more than an individual experience; it's been a catalyst for collective creativity and resilience. From Shakespeare's sonnets to Beyoncé's *Lemonade,* the art born from heartbreak connects us across generations, reminding us that we are never truly alone in our pain.

Heartbreak has also shaped societal attitudes towards love, teaching us to value vulnerability and connection. Each era's response to heartbreak reflects its unique cultural norms. Still, the underlying message remains the same: heartbreak is a shared human journey, one that has the power to transform us.

By examining heartbreak through the lens of history, we see that while the pain is deeply personal, its lessons are universal. Each era offers wisdom: the courage of ancient myths, the resilience of Roman stoicism, the creative beauty of medieval tales, the introspection of Victorian idealism, and the empowerment of modern narratives.

Let these stories inspire you. Heartbreak has shaped some of humanity's greatest art, literature, and philosophy achievements. Your story, too, has the potential to inspire transformation—not just for yourself but for others who may one day find solace in your strength.

As we continue this journey, remember that heartbreak is not the end of your story. It's a chapter in a narrative of resilience, growth, and boundless possibility.

Part II

Transforming Pain into Power

Chapter 5

Turning Pain into Power

Heartbreak is one of life's greatest inevitabilities. While viewing it as a setback is tempting, it can be a powerful force for transformation. When faced with emotional upheaval, the question isn't whether heartbreak will happen—but how we will respond to it. By confronting heartbreak with intention, we can uncover the strength we didn't know we had and emerge from the storm as stronger, more self-aware individuals.

In this chapter, we'll explore strategies for facing heartbreak head-on and transforming it into an opportunity for growth. Through real-life examples, we'll see how others have turned their pain into breakthroughs and learn actionable techniques to build resilience.

Before diving into strategies, reframing how we think about heartbreak is important. Instead of seeing it as a failure or an end, consider it a beginning—a chance to rebuild, redefine, and rediscover.

Think of heartbreak as a forest fire: while it burns fiercely, it clears space for new growth. By adopting this mindset, you shift from feeling powerless to empowered, ready to take control of your healing journey.

Mindset Shift Exercise: Write down one thing you've gained from this heartbreak. It might be clarity about what you need in a relationship or a deeper understanding of your resilience. Focusing on growth shifts your perspective from victimhood to empowerment.

Strategy 1: Mindfulness – Finding Calm Amid the Chaos

Heartbreak often brings a flood of overwhelming emotions. Mindfulness—being present at the moment without judgment—helps you navigate this emotional storm with greater clarity.

How to Practice Mindfulness

1. **Breathing Exercises:** When emotions feel intense, pause and focus on your breath.

   Inhale deeply for a count of four, hold for four, and exhale for six. This simple exercise calms your nervous system and brings you back to the present.

2. **Body Scans:** Lie down or sit comfortably, and focus on each part of your body, starting at your toes and moving upward. Notice any tension and release it as you exhale.
3. **Mindful Journaling:** Instead of analysing your feelings, write down your emotions as they come to you. Let the words flow without judgment. This practice creates space for self-reflection and emotional release.

After a painful divorce, Sarah turned to mindfulness to regain her footing. She started with short breathing exercises and gradually incorporated daily meditation. Over time, she found that mindfulness helped her manage the waves of sadness and rediscover a sense of peace.

Strategy 2: Creative Expression – Letting Emotions Take Shape

Heartbreak stirs a well of emotion that can feel overwhelming if left unexpressed. Creative outlets like writing, painting, music, or dance offer a safe way to process those feelings and transform them into something meaningful.

How to Get Started

1. **Write a Letter You'll Never Send:** Pour your feelings into a letter addressed to your ex or yourself. The goal isn't to deliver it but to articulate emotions that might otherwise stay bottled up.

2. **Create a Vision Board:** Use images, colours, and words to visualise your next chapter. This activity focuses your energy on the future, inspiring hope and motivation.
3. **Express Through Art:** Whether you sketch, paint, or sculpt, let your emotions guide your creation. You don't need to be an artist—this is about expression, not perfection.

When Miguel's long-term relationship ended, he felt lost. A friend encouraged him to pick up his old guitar. Writing songs about his pain became a lifeline, helping him process his emotions and eventually rediscover his passion for music.

Strategy 3: Building a Support Network

Heartbreak can feel isolating, but you don't have to face it alone. Leaning on others—whether friends, family, or support groups—provides encouragement and perspective that's hard to find on your own.

How to Build a Support Network

1. **Identify Your Support Circle:** List people you trust and feel comfortable talking to about your emotions.
2. **Join a Group:** Consider a support group, either in person or online, where you can share your experience with others going through similar challenges.

3. **Seek Professional Help:** A counselor or therapist can offer tools and insights tailored to your healing journey.

After her fiancé called off their engagement, Priya struggled with feelings of rejection. Joining a local support group for broken engagements gave her a sense of belonging. Hearing others' stories reminded her she wasn't alone, and their encouragement helped her move forward.

Strategy 4: Practicing Resilience

Resilience isn't about avoiding pain but bouncing back from it. Building resilience involves small, consistent actions that nurture your emotional well-being.

Steps to Cultivate Resilience

1. **Set Small Goals:** Start with manageable tasks, like cooking a new recipe or going for a walk. Each accomplishment boosts confidence and momentum.
2. **Focus on Self-Care:** Prioritise activities that replenish you, whether it's exercise, reading, or spending time with loved ones.
3. **Celebrate Progress:** Recognise and celebrate small wins, like a day when the sadness felt lighter or an evening spent smiling with friends.

John turned to running after a painful breakup. At first, it was just a way to distract himself, but over time, it became a metaphor for his recovery. Each mile he ran felt like a step closer to reclaiming his strength and independence.

Heartbreak will never be easy, but it can be transformative. By embracing strategies like mindfulness, creative expression, and support networks, you turn pain into an opportunity for growth. The stories of Sarah, Miguel, Priya, and John remind us that healing isn't just possible—it's inevitable when you approach it with intention and resilience.

This chapter is your invitation to take the first step toward empowerment. Heartbreak may have knocked you down, but the strength to rise, rebuild, and create a future filled with purpose and joy lies within you. Let the strategies here guide you as you step boldly into your next chapter.

Chapter 6

The Path to Healing

Healing from heartbreak can feel like standing at the base of a mountain, unsure of how to begin the climb. But every step you take is progress, bringing you closer to clarity, strength, and a renewed sense of self. This chapter offers a step-by-step guide to navigating the healing process, turning heartbreak into a transformative journey filled with opportunities for growth and self-discovery.

Each step is designed to be practical, actionable, and empowering, ensuring that you're not just moving on but moving forward.

Step 1: Acknowledge and Accept Your Emotions

The first step in healing is to confront your emotions

rather than suppress them. Heartbreak stirs a mix of feelings—sadness, anger, confusion, and even relief. Acknowledging these emotions without judgment is essential to processing them.

Exercise

1. Take 10 minutes each day to sit quietly with your thoughts. Name your emotions, like

   "I'm sad" or "I'm angry." This simple act of naming helps reduce their intensity.
2. Keep an "emotion journal," jot down your feelings and why. Over time, this practice brings clarity and helps you notice patterns.

Reflective Question: What emotions have I been avoiding, and how can I make space to feel them fully?

Step 2: Prioritise Self-Care

Heartbreak can leave you feeling drained, making self-care more critical than ever. Taking care of your body and mind creates the foundation for emotional recovery.

Practical Tips

- **Physical Care:** Start with small, manageable actions like drinking more water, eating nourishing meals, or walking. Exercise releases endorphins, helping you feel better.
- **Emotional Care:** Engage in activities that bring

comfort, whether it's reading, listening to music, or taking a relaxing bath.

- **Digital Detox:** Set boundaries with social media to avoid triggers like seeing your ex's posts. Use the time to focus on yourself instead.

Reflective Question: What simple, healthy habits can I incorporate into my daily routine to feel more balanced?

Step 3: Reflect and Learn

Reflection is a powerful tool for growth. Examining your relationship and its end can uncover valuable lessons that will guide you moving forward.

Exercise

- Write down three things you learned about yourself in the relationship.
- Reflect on what worked well and what didn't. Ask yourself, "What qualities do I want in future relationships?"
- Create a gratitude list, focusing on the positives you experienced. This isn't about romanticising the past but appreciating the good moments for what they were.

Reflective Question: How has this relationship shaped my understanding of love and myself?

Step 4: Rebuild Your Sense of Self

Heartbreak could shake your identity, especially if you tied a significant part of your self- worth to the relationship. This step is about rediscovering who you are outside of it.

Practical Tips

- **Reconnect with Passions:** Revisit hobbies or interests you may have set aside.

  Whether it's painting, hiking, or playing an instrument, doing what you love reaffirms your individuality.
- **Try Something New:** Sign up for a class, learn a skill, or explore a new interest. New experiences open doors to growth and excitement.
- **Set Personal Goals:** Focus on goals that are entirely about you—whether it's improving your fitness, starting a journal, or advancing your career.

Reflective Question: Who am I when this relationship does not define me, and what brings me joy?

Step 5: Strengthen Your Support System

Healing is easier when you surround yourself with people who care about you. Share your journey with trusted friends, family, or a support group.

Practical Tips

- Reach out to a friend and schedule regular check-ins. Having someone to talk to can lighten the burden.

- Consider joining a local or online community of individuals experiencing similar challenges. Knowing you're not alone can be incredibly reassuring.
- Don't hesitate to seek professional support if needed. A counselor or therapist can provide guidance tailored to your needs.

Reflective Question: Who in my life supports me, and how can I lean on them during this time?

Step 6: Embrace Renewal

The final stage is about moving forward with intention. Renewal doesn't mean forgetting the past—it means carrying its lessons into a brighter future.

Exercise

- Create a vision board for the next chapter of your life. Include images, words, and symbols representing your goals, dreams, and values.
- Write a letter to your future self detailing how you hope to feel and what you aim to achieve six months or a year from now.
- Commit to small, actionable steps towards your goals. Celebrate each milestone, no matter how small.

Reflective Question: What does a fulfilling, joyful future look like for me, and how can I start building it today?

Healing isn't a straight line—it's a winding path with ups and downs. Some days will feel easier than others, and that's okay. The important thing is to keep moving forward, trusting that every small step brings you closer to wholeness.

By acknowledging your emotions, caring for yourself, reflecting on your experiences, and embracing renewal, you're not just overcoming heartbreak but transforming it into a powerful catalyst for growth.

Remember, this journey isn't about erasing the past; it's about using it to build a stronger, wiser, and more compassionate version of yourself. You are capable of incredible resilience and beauty, and this path to healing is just the beginning of a brighter, more fulfilling chapter in your life.

Let each step remind you that you are not broken—you are becoming.

Chapter 7

Letting Go of the Unchangeable

"Is it possible to control the past?" On the surface, the answer is simple: no. But for anyone who has experienced heartbreak, the question feels more complex. We replay conversations, second-guess decisions, and cling to believing that the outcome could have changed if we had done something differently. These thoughts often trap us in a cycle of regret, draining our emotional energy and robbing us of peace.

This chapter explores why we try to control the past, why it's impossible, and how to let go of the exhausting struggle of *what ifs* and *if onlys*. By embracing the unchangeable nature of the past, we free ourselves to live fully in the present and invest in a future brimming with possibility.

Our desire to control the past stems from a natural human instinct: the need to make sense of pain. When heartbreak occurs, our minds look for reasons, replaying events to find answers. This can lead to thoughts like:

- *"If only I had tried harder."*
- *"What if I had noticed the signs earlier?"*
- *"If they hadn't said that, things might be different."*

These questions create the illusion that, with enough effort, we could rewrite history. But the truth is, the past is beyond our reach. Holding onto these thoughts is like trying to grasp water—it slips through your fingers, leaving you empty and frustrated.

Reflective Question: What are the "if onlys" and "what ifs" you keep revisiting, and how do they impact your peace of mind?

Trying to control the past isn't just futile—it's exhausting. It keeps you emotionally tethered to a moment that no longer exists, preventing you from moving forward. The mental energy spent reliving old scenarios could be used to build something new and meaningful in your life.

Consider this: When you argue with the unchangeable, you give your power to something that can't respond or change. This struggle creates unnecessary suffering, leaving little room for joy, creativity, or hope.

Exercise

Imagine you're holding a rope tied to a heavy boulder (your past). Every time you replay regrets, you're pulling on that rope, expending energy. Visualise yourself letting go of the rope. Feel the release. Practice this mental exercise whenever you feel stuck in the past.

Letting go of the past doesn't mean dismissing it or pretending it didn't matter. Instead, it's about acknowledging its place in your story and allowing it to remain in the past, where it belongs. Embracing reality is an act of grace—towards yourself and the situation.

1. **Acceptance Doesn't Mean Approval:** You don't have to agree with what happened to accept it. Acceptance simply means recognising that the past can't be undone.
2. **Redefine Your Relationship with the Past:** Instead of seeing the past as a source of regret, view it as a teacher. What lessons can you carry forward?

Reflective Question: How can I shift my perspective to see the past as a learning experience rather than a weight to carry?

Letting go of the past requires intentional action. Here are practical steps to free yourself from the struggle of trying to rewrite history:

1. **Create a "Done" List**

   Write down the events or decisions you've been holding onto. Next to each, write, "This is done. I release it." Repeat this process whenever regrets arise, reinforcing your commitment to letting go.

2. **Focus on the Controllable**

   Shift your energy to what you can influence: your mindset, your actions, and your future. Create a list of goals or dreams that excite you and take one small step toward them each day.

3. **Practice the Power of "And"**

   Let two truths coexist: "I wish things had been different and I accept that they weren't." This practice bridges the gap between longing and acceptance, making it easier to move forward.

4. **Establish a Letting-Go Ritual**

   Find a symbolic way to release your regrets. Write them on a piece of paper and tear it up or burn it (safely). Visualise the past dissolving, leaving you lighter and freer.

Exercise

Each night, reflect on your day and identify one thought or regret you're ready to release. Say aloud, "I let go of [insert regret]. I choose peace."

When you stop fighting the past, you open yourself to future possibilities. Letting go creates emotional and mental space for joy, growth, and connection. It allows you to focus on what truly matters—your values, your dreams, and the person you're becoming.

Imagine your life as a garden. The past is the soil—rich with lessons and experiences. But the future is where you plant seeds, nurture growth, and watch beauty unfold. You can't change the soil, but you can choose what you plant and how you care for it.

Reflective Question: What seeds do I want to plant for the future, and how can I nurture them today?

Releasing the need to control the past isn't about giving up—it's about reclaiming your power. It's a declaration that your future is more important than dwelling on what can't be changed.

Remember, the past is part of your story but doesn't define your entire narrative. By letting go, you're writing the next chapter with intention, creativity, and hope.

As you continue this journey, remind yourself: You are not bound by the past. You can grow, heal, and create a future filled with purpose and possibility. Let the act of letting go be your greatest gift to yourself—a gift of freedom, clarity, and boundless potential.

Chapter 8

Creating Space for Growth

Unburdening yourself from the past is not about forgetting—it's about lightening your emotional load, making room for new experiences and personal growth. The past, while unchangeable, doesn't have to define your present or dictate your future. You can find peace and clarity by identifying the emotional ties that anchor you, reflecting on their meaning, and developing practices to gradually release them.

This chapter guides confronting attachments, recognising triggers, and implementing strategies that help you move towards liberation and renewal. The absence of memories doesn't define success, but it is declined by the increasing moments of inner peace and freedom, you experience.

Step 1: Identify What's Holding You Back

The first step in letting go is understanding what keeps you tethered to the past. Emotional ties can take many forms—unresolved feelings, recurring memories, or attachments to unexpected outcomes.

Exercise to Identify Emotional Ties

1. Take a quiet moment to sit with your thoughts. Close your eyes and ask yourself, "What keeps coming back to me when I think about the past?"
2. Write down your responses. These could be specific memories, feelings of regret, or unresolved conversations.
3. Label each tie as either an emotion (e.g., guilt, longing) or a thought pattern (e.g., "I should have done this differently").

Reflective Question: What am I holding onto, and why do I feel it's challenging to let go?

Step 2: Confront Attachments Through Reflection

Reflection allows you to explore your attachments with curiosity and compassion. Rather than judging yourself for holding on, focus on understanding why these ties persist and their purpose.

Guided Reflection Exercise

- Write about each emotional tie you've identified.

Answer these questions:

- Why is this significant to me?
- What am I afraid of losing if I let this go?
- How does holding onto this tie affect my well-being?

- Reflect on patterns that emerge. Do certain thoughts or emotions recur?

This process helps you uncover the deeper reasons behind your attachments, giving you clarity and a sense of direction.

Reflective Question: What have I learned about myself from exploring my attachments?

Step 3: Gradual Detachment Through Intentional Practices

Detaching from the past doesn't happen overnight—it's a gradual process that requires patience and intentional effort. By engaging in practices that encourage emotional release, you allow yourself to loosen the grip of the past.

Practical Techniques for Detachment

1. **Journaling:** Write a daily or weekly reflection about your emotions and progress.
   Include affirmations like, "I am choosing to let go, little by little."

2. **Meditation:** Use guided meditations focused on release and renewal. Visualise the emotional ties dissolving with each exhale.
3. **Creative Expression:** Whether it's painting, writing poetry, or playing music, channel your emotions into something creative. This helps externalise what you're feeling, making it easier to process.
4. **Set an Intention:** Begin each day with an affirmation like, "Today, I will focus on creating space for joy and growth."

Reflective Question: What practice feels most natural for me to start with, and how can I commit to it regularly?

Step 4: Recognising and Managing Triggers

As you work to detach from the past, certain triggers will inevitably arise. Triggers are reminders—places, people, or situations—that bring unresolved emotions back to the surface. Instead of fearing them, view triggers as opportunities to practice resilience.

How to Recognise Triggers

- Pay attention to moments when strong emotions resurface.
- Reflect on what brought those emotions up—was it a specific place, song, or conversation?

Strategies to Manage Triggers

1. **Pause and Acknowledge:** When a trigger arises, pause and say, "I recognise this feeling. It's okay to feel this way." This validation helps you stay present.
2. **Shift Your Focus:** Engage in an activity that grounds you, like taking a walk, drinking a glass of water, or practicing deep breathing.
3. **Create Boundaries:** Limit exposure to situations or reminders that consistently provoke emotional distress.

Reflective Question: What triggers have I identified, and how can I respond to them in a way that supports my well-being?

Step 5: Measuring Progress Through Peace and Clarity

Progress in letting go isn't about completely forgetting the past—it's about noticing when its hold on you begins to fade. These moments of peace and clarity signal that you're moving forward.

Signs of Progress

- You spend less time thinking about the past.
- Triggers feel less intense and easier to navigate.
- You feel lighter and more focused on the present.
- You notice an increase in joy and curiosity about the future.

Celebrate Small Wins

- At the end of each day, reflect on one moment where you felt free or at peace.

  Acknowledge this as a sign of growth.
- Reward yourself for reaching milestones, like journaling consistently for a month or successfully managing a difficult trigger.

Reflective Question: How can I celebrate the moments of peace and clarity I've achieved so far?

Letting go of the past isn't about erasing your history—it's about creating space for a new, vibrant chapter in your life. As you detach from what no longer serves you, you open the door to new opportunities, relationships, and experiences.

Remember, this process is uniquely yours. It doesn't need to follow a specific timeline or look a certain way. No matter how small, each step you take is a step towards freedom.

You are reclaiming your energy and focus by identifying your emotional ties, reflecting on their meaning, and practicing detachment. You are not just leaving the past behind—you are stepping forward into a future filled with potential and growth.

This journey is a testament to your strength and resilience. As you continue, let each moment of clarity remind you of the limitless possibilities that await a heart unburdened by the weight of yesterday. You are free to grow, thrive, and embrace the beautiful life ahead of you.

Chapter 9

Stories of Strength: Real-Life Journeys of Letting Go

The process of letting go is a deeply personal journey, yet it connects us across cultures, backgrounds, and experiences. Each story of acceptance is unique, shaped by individual circumstances, yet they all share a common thread: the courage to move forward.

In this chapter, we explore real-life narratives of people who faced the daunting task of letting go after heartbreak. These case studies inspire and provide practical insights into how others have navigated their journey. Their stories remind us that while letting go may feel insurmountable, it is entirely possible—and often transformative.

Aditi's Story: Finding Strength in Routine (India)

Aditi's seven-year relationship ended abruptly, leaving her feeling lost and untethered. She described her heartbreak as "a void that consumed everything." Initially, she struggled to imagine life without the partnership she had built.

Challenge: Aditi found herself stuck in a cycle of rumination, replaying the breakup in her mind and questioning her own worth.

Strategy: Inspired by the concept of *sadhana*—a disciplined practice in Indian culture—Aditi created a daily routine to ground herself. She started each morning with yoga and journaling, using these moments to reconnect with her body and mind. She would take long walks in the evenings, allowing herself to process her emotions in the open air.

Outcome: Over time, Aditi's routine gave her a sense of stability and purpose. "It didn't erase the pain," she said, "but it gave me a way to coexist with it while moving forward."

Takeaway: Establishing a daily routine can provide structure and a sense of control during periods of emotional turmoil.

James's Story: The Healing Power of Nature (Canada)

James, an outdoor enthusiast from Canada, had always felt at home in the wilderness. But after his marriage ended, the natural landscapes he loved seemed lifeless and gray.

Challenge: James struggled with feelings of failure and shame, believing he hadn't done enough to save his marriage. These emotions made it difficult for him to return to his beloved hiking trails.

Strategy: A friend encouraged James to revisit nature, not as a place of escape but as a space for healing. He began taking short, mindful hikes, focusing on the sights, sounds, and smells around him. He also started carrying a sketchbook, capturing the beauty he saw along the way.

Outcome: Reconnecting with nature allowed James to see his pain as part of a larger cycle. "The changing seasons reminded me that nothing stays the same forever," he shared. His sketches became a visual journal of his healing journey.

Takeaway: Immersing yourself in nature can offer perspective and a sense of renewal. It reminds us of the impermanence of all things, including pain.

Maria's Story: Letting Go Through Storytelling (Mexico)

For Maria, a teacher and writer from Mexico, storytelling had always been a way to make sense of the world. After her long-term partner left her, she felt an overwhelming need to give voice to her experience.

Challenge: Maria wrestled with feelings of

rejection and a loss of identity. "I didn't know who I was without this relationship," she admitted.

Strategy: She began writing short stories based on her emotions. At first, the characters in her stories mirrored her own pain, but gradually, they grew into resilient individuals who found peace and joy. Sharing her stories with friends and eventually publishing them online helped Maria feel connected and empowered.

Outcome: Storytelling gave Maria a way to process her emotions and redefine herself. "Writing let me imagine a version of myself that was whole—and then I became her," she said.

Takeaway: Creative expression, such as writing, can be a powerful tool for processing emotions and reimagining your future.

Ahmed's Story: Building Community for Healing (Egypt)

When Ahmed's engagement ended, he felt isolated in his heartbreak. "In my culture, men don't talk about these things," he explained. "It was lonely."

Challenge: Ahmed's inability to share his feelings openly led to bottled-up emotions that manifested as anxiety and anger.

Strategy: Realising he wasn't alone, Ahmed started a local support group for men dealing with emotional challenges. The group met weekly, providing a safe space for open conversations about heartbreak, grief, and mental health.

Outcome: Leading the group helped Ahmed process his feelings and gave him a sense of purpose. "Helping others heal healed me," he said.

Takeaway: Building or joining a supportive community can provide connection, understanding, and shared growth during difficult times.

Hana's Story: Rediscovering Self-Love (South Korea)

Hana, an artist from South Korea, always prioritised her partner's needs over hers. When their relationship ended, she realised how much of herself she had lost.

Challenge: Hana felt disconnected from her identity and unsure how to move forward.

Strategy: She embarked on a journey of self-discovery, taking solo trips to places she had always wanted to visit. She also began painting self-portraits, exploring how she saw herself at different stages of her healing.

Outcome: Hana's travels and artwork helped her rebuild her sense of self. "I learned to enjoy my own company," she reflected. "And I fell in love with the person I am."

Takeaway: Prioritising self-love and self-discovery can help you reconnect with who you are beyond the relationship.

Lessons from These Stories

The journeys of Aditi, James, Maria, Ahmed, and Hana

remind us that letting go is not about forgetting or erasing—it's about transforming. Each person faced unique challenges, employed different strategies, and found healing in their own way.

Universal Insights

- Letting go requires patience and self-compassion.
- Healing often involves both solitary reflection and meaningful connection.
- Creative expression, physical movement, and mindfulness are powerful tools for emotional release.

As you navigate your journey, remember that you have the strength to move forward. Let these stories serve as a reminder that you are not alone—and that the path to healing is as unique as you are.

Take inspiration from these individuals, but don't feel pressured to follow their exact steps. Your story is yours to write; every moment of progress is a testament to your resilience and courage.

Letting go is not the end—it's the beginning of a new chapter filled with growth, possibility, and the limitless potential to create a life you love.

Part III

Embracing Acceptance and Renewal

Chapter 10

Embracing the Emotional Mosaic

Heartbreak is rarely defined by just one emotion. It's a complex mosaic, with each feeling—be it sadness, anger, relief, or hope—representing a distinct part of the healing journey. These emotions may seem overwhelming at times, but each one plays a vital role in moving forward.

In this chapter, we'll explore how to embrace these feelings without judgment, allowing them to flow naturally and transform into stepping stones rather than stumbling blocks. Understanding and accepting your emotional landscape prepares you to step into a more resilient, empowered version of yourself.

When heartbreak strikes, emotions often arrive in waves. Some are expected—sadness, anger, or regret—while others, like relief or hope, might surprise you. Understanding these emotions as part of a larger picture helps you navigate them with greater clarity and compassion.

Sadness: Sadness is the natural response to loss, a reflection of how deeply you cared. While it may feel all-consuming, sadness is essential to the healing process. It allows you to honour what was while making room for what can be.

Anger: Anger can be energising, pushing you to confront injustices or unmet expectations. While it's important not to let anger consume you, it can also serve as a motivator for setting boundaries and advocating for yourself.

Relief: Relief might feel like a strange companion in heartbreak, but it often emerges when you recognise that the relationship was no longer serving you. Embrace relief as a sign that you are beginning to see possibilities beyond the pain.

Hope: Hope is the light that appears when you start to believe in a future unbound by heartbreak. It doesn't negate your pain but coexists with it, reminding you that brighter days are ahead.

Reflective Question: Which emotions do I experience most often, and how can I honour them without judgment?

One of the most challenging aspects of heartbreak is the temptation to suppress emotions. It's natural to want to avoid discomfort, but bottling up feelings only delays healing. Instead, practice allowing your emotions to flow naturally.

Practical Ways to Embrace Your Emotions

1. **Name Your Feelings:** When an emotion arises, name it. For example, "I feel sadness right now" or "This is anger." Acknowledging emotions helps diminish their intensity.
2. **Give Yourself Time and Space:** Dedicate specific moments in your day to sit with your emotions. This could be through journaling, meditating, or simply being still.
3. **Talk It Out:** Share your feelings with someone you trust, whether it's a friend, family member, or therapist. Verbalising emotions can bring clarity and relief.

Reflective Question: How can I create space in my life to experience and process my emotions fully?

Each emotion has something to teach you. When you approach your feelings with curiosity rather than judgement, they become tools for growth rather than obstacles.

Sadness as a Teacher: Sadness encourages introspection, helping you understand what truly matters to you. Reflect on the values and needs the relationship revealed, and carry these insights into your future.

Anger as a Boundary-Setter: Anger can help you identify areas where your boundaries were crossed. Use this energy to establish healthier limits moving forward, whether in relationships or in your own expectations.

Relief as Permission: Relief permits you to envision life beyond the relationship. Let it guide you toward new possibilities, reminding you that endings are also beginnings.

Hope as Motivation: Hope fuels resilience, encouraging you to take small steps towards a brighter future. Use this emotion to set goals, whether they're personal, professional, or relational.

Reflective Question: What lessons can I learn from the emotions I've experienced during this journey?

Accepting your emotions also requires extending compassion to yourself. It's easy to judge your feelings—thinking you're too emotional, angry, or slow to heal. But every emotion is valid, and every person heals at their own pace.

Self-Compassion Practices

1. **Positive Self-Talk:** Replace critical thoughts with affirming ones, such as, "It's okay to feel this way," or "I'm doing my best."
2. **Physical Comfort:** Place your hand over your heart or hug yourself when emotions feel overwhelming. These small gestures can be grounding and soothing.

3. **Celebrate Small Wins:** Acknowledge the moments when you honour your feelings, no matter how small. Progress is worth celebrating.

Reflective Question: How can I treat myself with kindness during moments of emotional intensity?

As you learn to embrace your emotions, you'll notice subtle shifts that signal your progress:

- You begin to accept feelings as they come without trying to suppress or control them.
- Triggers become less overwhelming, and you recover more quickly when they arise.
- You experience moments of peace and gratitude alongside the more challenging emotions.
- You start to believe in your capacity to heal and grow.

Reflective Question: What signs of resilience have I noticed in myself recently?

The mosaic of emotions that accompanies heartbreak is not a barrier—it's a bridge. By embracing each feeling as part of your journey, you build a path towards resilience and self-awareness. Every emotion, no matter how difficult, contributes to your growth.

This process is not about perfection—it's about presence. It's about showing up for yourself, honouring your feelings, and trusting that each step forward brings you closer to a life unburdened by the past.

Remember, resilience isn't about avoiding pain; it's about learning to navigate it with grace and strength. As you continue to embrace your emotional landscape, you're not just healing-you're transforming. And with each piece of the mosaic, you create a picture of a life filled with clarity, strength, and endless possibilities.

Chapter 11

Acceptance as the Gateway to Transformation

Acceptance is not the final chapter of healing—it's the doorway to something greater. Like a chrysalis cradling a caterpillar before it becomes a butterfly, acceptance provides a space for profound transformation. It allows you to shed the weight of the past, discover newfound strength, and emerge ready to redefine your future.

In this chapter, we'll explore how embracing acceptance fosters inner peace and clarity, empowering you to rewrite your life's narrative. We'll also compare the paths of those who accept their reality with those who resist it, illustrating the profound difference acceptance makes in shaping your life's trajectory.

Think of acceptance as a chrysalis—a protective

cocoon that nurtures growth. When you embrace acceptance, you create an environment where healing and transformation can take place. This stage isn't passive; it's an active process of reflection, release, and renewal.

Like the caterpillar that dissolves and reforms within the chrysalis, acceptance involves letting go of what no longer serves you and reconstructing your sense of self. It's not about forgetting the past but using it as a foundation for growth.

Reflective Question: What parts of myself or my past do I need to release to make space for transformation?

One of the greatest gifts of acceptance is the inner peace it brings. When you stop resisting what cannot be changed, you free yourself from the emotional turmoil of "what ifs" and "if onlys." This clarity allows you to focus on what truly matters—your present and your future.

How to Cultivate Peace and Clarity

1. **Mindful Presence:** Practice being fully present in the moment. Use mindfulness techniques to anchor yourself in the here and now, such as focusing on your breath or engaging with your surroundings.
2. **Gratitude Practice:** Reflect on the lessons and strengths you've gained through your journey. Gratitude shifts your focus from loss to abundance.

3. **Simplify Your Priorities:** Let go of distractions or obligations that no longer align with your values. Clarity emerges when you focus on what truly matters.

Reflective Question: What steps can I take today to invite more peace and clarity into my life?

Acceptance is the gateway to rewriting your story. No longer defined by heartbreak or loss, you can craft a new narrative that centres on resilience, purpose, and possibility.

How to Redefine Your Life's Narrative

- **Set New Intentions:** Reflect on what you want to create in this new chapter of your life. What brings you joy, fulfillment, and purpose?
- **Envision Your Future:** Create a vision board or describe your ideal life five years from now. Include everything that inspires you, from relationships to personal achievements.
- **Embrace Your Strengths:** Recognise the qualities that have carried you through heartbreak. Let these strengths guide your next steps.

Reflective Question: What story do I want to tell about this chapter of my life, and how can I start living it today?

The choice to embrace or resist acceptance shapes

your life in profound ways. While resistance keeps you tethered to the past, acceptance propels you forward, opening the door to transformation.

Those Who Resist Acceptance

- Often feel stuck, replaying old memories or regrets.
- Struggle with emotional turmoil, as resistance amplifies pain and prolongs healing.
- Miss opportunities for growth, as energy is spent clinging to the past rather than building the future.

Those Who Embrace Acceptance

- Experience emotional freedom, as they release the weight of what cannot be changed.
- Develop clarity and purpose, focusing on what they can control.
- Open themselves to new opportunities and relationships, unencumbered by past shadows.

Case Study

- **Resisting Acceptance:** Lena spent years replaying her breakup, unable to move on because she clung to the hope of reconciliation. Her energy was drained by her inability to let go, leaving little room for joy or growth.
- **Embracing Acceptance:** In contrast, Alex chose to accept his heartbreak, focusing on his personal

growth. He pursued new hobbies, deepened his relationships with friends, and eventually found a renewed sense of purpose. Alex's life flourished because he embraced acceptance as a catalyst for transformation.

Reflective Question: Am I resisting or embracing acceptance, and how is this choice shaping my journey?

Acceptance is not the end of the road; it's the beginning of a journey towards a brighter, more purposeful future. To harness its transformative power, set clear intentions for the life you want to create.

Steps to Set Intentions

1. **Reflect on Your Values:** What matters most to you? Use these values as a compass to guide your decisions.
2. **Create a Roadmap:** Break down your intentions into actionable steps. For example, if your goal is to build meaningful connections, start by reaching out to a friend or joining a community group.
3. **Celebrate Progress:** Acknowledge each step you take, no matter how small.

   Progress is worth celebrating.

Reflective Question: What intentions can I set today to begin creating a life aligned with my values and aspirations?

Just as the butterfly emerges from the chrysalis, so too can you emerge from acceptance transformed. This process is not about erasing your past but about integrating it into a narrative of strength and resilience.

By embracing acceptance, you create space for inner peace, clarity, and a renewed sense of purpose. You are no longer bound by heartbreak or loss—you are free to grow, to create, and to thrive.

Remember, acceptance is not the end of your story—it's the beginning of a new chapter filled with possibility, purpose, and the potential to become the best version of yourself. The gateway is open. Step through with courage and embrace the extraordinary transformation that awaits.

Chapter 12

Surrendering to the Current of Acceptance

Acceptance is the foundation upon which healing from heartbreak is built. It's not about giving up but about surrendering to a gentle current that carries you towards peace. Like floating in the ocean, acceptance allows you to stop fighting against the waves and instead move with them, trusting they will guide you to calmer waters.

In this chapter, we'll define acceptance, explore its emotional landscapes, and dispel common misconceptions. By understanding the transformative power of acceptance, you can release self-blame, free yourself from the grip of "what might have been," and begin your journey towards a lighter heart and a brighter future.

Acceptance is often misunderstood as resignation or defeat, but it's neither. True acceptance is an active choice to acknowledge reality as it is, without resistance or denial. It doesn't mean you approve of what happened or that the pain disappears—it means you've stopped fighting against the unchangeable.

Acceptance is an act of empowerment. By choosing to let go of resistance, you reclaim your energy and focus, directing it towards healing and growth rather than the impossible task of rewriting the past.

Reflective Question: How can I embrace the reality of my situation without feeling like I'm giving up?

The journey to acceptance is not linear. It's a winding path through a rich emotional landscape, each feeling playing a vital role in the process:

1. **Acknowledgment:** The first step in acceptance is acknowledging your pain and the reality of the situation. This may feel heavy, but it's necessary to move forward.
2. **Relief:** Once you stop resisting the truth, a sense of relief often follows. The energy you once spent fighting the past becomes available for healing.
3. **Clarity:** Acceptance brings a clearer perspective. You begin to see the situation for what it is, rather than through the lens of regret or wishful thinking.

4. **Hope:** With clarity comes hope. Acceptance opens the door to new possibilities and the realisation that life can still be fulfilling.

Reflective Question: Which emotions have I encountered on my journey towards acceptance, and how have they shaped my perspective?

Many people resist acceptance because of misconceptions about what it means. Let's dispel some of these myths:

- **Myth 1: Acceptance Equals Approval**

Truth: Acceptance doesn't mean you condone what happened. It means you acknowledge that it cannot be undone and choose to move forward.

- **Myth 2: Acceptance Means Forgetting**

Truth: Acceptance is not about erasing memories or pretending the past didn't happen. It's about integrating those experiences into your story without letting them define you.

- **Myth 3: Acceptance Is Weakness**

Truth: Acceptance requires strength and courage. It's a bold step toward taking control of your emotional well-being.

Reflective Question: What misconceptions about acceptance might be holding me back, and how can I reframe them?

Liberation Through Acceptance: One of the most profound gifts of acceptance is liberation. When you let go of self-blame and the longing for what could have been, you free yourself from emotional shackles.

Liberation from Self-Blame: Heartbreak often leads to self-blame as you replay scenarios and question your decisions. Acceptance reminds you that relationships are complex and that responsibility rarely lies with one person alone.

Liberation from 'What Might Have Been': The "what ifs" and "if onlys" can keep you trapped in a cycle of regret. Acceptance allows you to release these thoughts, recognising that they only drain your energy without changing the past.

Reflective Question: What would it feel like to release self-blame and stop dwelling on what might have been?

Acceptance doesn't just help you heal—it transforms how you see yourself and your future. It shifts your perspective, allowing you to focus on what you can create rather than what you've lost.

- **Shifting Perspectives:** Acceptance helps you see challenges as opportunities for growth. You stop viewing heartbreak as the end and start seeing it as a new beginning.
- **Paving the Way for Growth:** By letting go of resistance, you make room for personal growth, new relationships, and meaningful experiences.
- **Creating a Lighter Heart:** Acceptance lightens

your emotional load, making it easier to move forward with joy and purpose.

Reflective Question: How has my perspective shifted as I've worked towards acceptance, and what new possibilities have I discovered?

Acceptance sets the stage for the next phase of healing: letting go. With a clear and open heart, you can begin to release the attachments that no longer serve you, making space for new experiences and opportunities.

Practical Steps Towards Letting Go

1. **Daily Affirmations:** Repeat affirmations like, "I accept my past and embrace my future."
2. **Mindful Reflection:** Spend a few minutes each day reflecting on how far you've come and your progress.
3. **Future-Focused Intentions:** Write down one thing you're looking forward to, no matter how small.

Reflective Question: What steps can I take today to begin building a future unburdened by my past?

Acceptance is not a destination—it's a gateway. By embracing it, you free yourself from the chains of resistance and step into a space of possibility and transformation.

This process requires patience and self-compassion. There may be moments when old feelings resurface, but each time you choose acceptance, you strengthen your resilience and reclaim your peace.

Remember, the journey of healing doesn't end with acceptance-it begins there. It's the foundation for a life filled with growth, joy, and endless potential. By surrendering to the current of acceptance, you're not just healing-you're transforming, and the best is yet to come.

Part IV

Reconnecting With Your Inner Self

Chapter 13

Rekindling Your Inner Flame Through Core Values

Rediscovering your inner flame after heartbreak involves more than just moving on—it requires looking inward, reconnecting with your true self, and understanding what truly drives you. At the heart of this journey lies your core values. These values act as a compass, guiding your decisions, shaping your relationships, and helping you find fulfillment.

In this chapter, we'll define core values, explore their significance in personal growth, and reflect on their role in rediscovering your authentic self. Integrating your values into your daily life can illuminate a path towards healing, purpose, and joy.

Core values are the fundamental beliefs that guide

your actions and decisions. They reflect what matters most to you—principles like integrity, compassion, freedom, or growth. These values serve as a framework for how you navigate the world, influencing how you treat others, handle challenges, and pursue your goals.

Why Core Values Matter

- **Anchor in Uncertainty:** Core values provide stability during times of change, helping you make decisions that align with who you are.
- **Source of Motivation:** When your actions align with your values, you feel more energised and fulfilled.
- **Foundation for Authenticity:** Living by your values allows you to stay true to yourself, even when faced with external pressures.

Reflective Question: What principles do I hold close to my heart, and how do they influence my life?

Understanding your values often involves reflecting on pivotal life experiences. These moments reveal what truly matters to you, whether joyful or challenging.

Exercise

1. Think about a time when you felt deeply fulfilled. What were you doing? Who were you with? What values were at play?

2. Now reflect on a moment of conflict or discomfort. What value was being challenged or unmet?
3. Write down the values that emerge from these reflections. These might include honesty, kindness, independence, or creativity.

Example

- **Moment of Fulfillment:** Kanika felt most alive while volunteering at an animal shelter.

  This experience highlighted her core values of compassion and service.
- **Moment of Conflict:** Kanika struggled in a work environment where honesty was not prioritised, emphasising the importance of integrity in her life.

Reflective Question: What experiences have shaped my understanding of what I value most?

Core values are universal in their application, often aligning with timeless concepts like integrity, compassion, and perseverance. Let's explore these parallels:

- **Integrity:** Living in alignment with your values fosters a sense of self-respect and trust. When your actions match your beliefs, you feel grounded and authentic.
- **Compassion:** Valuing empathy and kindness strengthens your relationships and deepens your connection to others.

- **Perseverance:** Holding onto values like resilience and determination helps you overcome challenges and stay focused on your goals.

Reflective Question: Which well-known concepts resonate with my core values, and how can I fully embody them?

To fully rediscover your inner flame, assessing your current values and how they influence your daily life is essential.

Steps to Identify Your Core Values

1. **Create a List:** Write down all the values that come to mind. You can use prompts like, "What qualities do I admire in others?" or "What makes me feel most fulfilled?"
2. **Narrow It Down:** Choose your top five values. These are the principles that resonate most deeply with you.
3. **Reflect on Alignment:** Assess how well your current lifestyle aligns with these values. Are there areas where you're living in alignment? Are there areas where you're not?

Maria identified her top values as family, honesty, creativity, independence, and growth. She realised that while her family relationships reflected these values, her career didn't provide opportunities for creativity or growth.

Reflective Question: How aligned is my current life with my core values, and where can I make adjustments?

Once you've identified your values, the next step is to integrate them into your daily decisions. This alignment creates a sense of purpose and fulfillment.

Practical Ways to Live Your Values

1. **Set Value-Driven Goals:** Use your values to guide your goals. For example, if health is a core value, set a goal to exercise regularly or eat mindfully.
2. **Make Conscious Choices:** Ask yourself, "Does this align with my values?"
3. **Reflect Regularly:** At the end of each day, reflect on how your actions aligned with your values and where you could improve.

Reflective Question: What steps can I take today to ensure my actions reflect my core values?

Rediscovering your inner flame isn't just about healing—it's about growing into the best version of yourself. Core values play a pivotal role in this transformation by:

- **Clarifying Your Purpose:** Knowing your values helps identify what truly fulfills you.
- **Strengthening Your Confidence:** Living by your values builds self-trust and reinforces your identity.

- **Enhancing Your Relationships:** When you align your values with your actions, you attract people and opportunities that resonate with your authentic self.

Reflective Question: How have my core values shaped the person I am today, and how can they guide my future?

Rediscovering your inner flame begins with understanding and honouring your core values. These principles are your guide, lighting the way through the darkness of heartbreak and into a future filled with purpose and possibility.

By reflecting on your values, aligning your actions with them, and embracing their transformative power, you set the stage for a life that feels authentic, fulfilling, and uniquely yours. Remember, your inner flame has always been there—this journey is about reigniting it, one value-driven step at a time.

Chapter 14

Reawakening Your Passions

Imagine a garden in the quiet of winter, the seeds lying dormant beneath the soil, waiting for the warmth of spring to coax them back to life. Much like this garden, our passions often gets buried under the weight of heartbreak, hidden but not gone. The journey of healing isn't just about letting go of pain—it's about reawakening the joy, creativity, and purpose that make life vibrant.

In this chapter, we explore how to uncover and nurture your passions, using the story of one individual who transformed grief into a renewed love for art. By reconnecting with past joys and embracing new experiences, you, too can cultivate your inner garden, allowing your passions to bloom once more.

Heartbreak has a way of overshadowing the things that once brought us joy. Activities that used to light us up can feel distant, their spark extinguished by the weight of sadness. But just like seeds lying dormant in the soil, your passions are still there, waiting for the right conditions to reemerge.

Recognising that your passions haven't disappeared—they've simply been overshadowed—is the first step in reconnecting with them.

Reflective Question: What activities or interests used to bring me joy, and how might I begin to revisit them?

Case Study: Anna's Journey Back to Art

Anna was a graphic designer who had always loved painting. But when she lost her partner unexpectedly, her brushes gathered dust, and her canvases lay untouched. "I couldn't see the point," she said. "Everything felt hollow."

After months of grieving, Anna's therapist encouraged her to revisit painting, not as a means to create something beautiful but as a way to express her emotions. Hesitant at first, Anna began painting abstract shapes, pouring her feelings onto the canvas without worrying about the outcome.

This simple act of reconnecting with her passion sparked something in Anna. Over time, her paintings became more vibrant, reflecting her journey from grief to renewal. Her art became a bridge between her pain and healing, helping her rediscover her creativity and her sense of self.

Lesson from Anna's Story: Revisiting a passion can serve as both an emotional outlet and a pathway to rediscovering your identity.

Strategies for Reawakening Your Passions

Reigniting your passions doesn't happen overnight—it's a gradual process of exploration and experimentation. Here are practical strategies to help you reconnect with what lights you up:

1. **Start Small:** Begin with something manageable, like dedicating 10 minutes a day to your hobby. For example, if you love writing, jot down a few thoughts or ideas without pressuring yourself to produce something "perfect."
2. **Reconnect with Past Joys:** Reflect on activities that brought you happiness in the past. Did you love baking, gardening, or dancing? Revisit those interests, even if it feels unfamiliar at first.
3. **Embrace New Experiences:** Sometimes, heartbreak opens the door to exploring new passions. Sign up for a class, try a new sport, or attend a workshop that piques your curiosity.
4. **Use Passion as an Emotional Outlet:** Treat your passions as a way to process emotions. Whether through painting, journaling, or playing music, channel your feelings into your chosen activity.

Reflective Question: What small step can I take today to begin reconnecting with an old or new passion?

The power of passion lies in its ability to transform pain into purpose. When you engage with something you love, it reminds you of your capacity for joy and creativity, even in the midst of challenges. Passion doesn't erase grief, but it offers a way to integrate it into your growth journey.

Signs You're Reawakening Your Passion

- You lose track of time while engaged in your activity.
- You feel a sense of accomplishment, regardless of the outcome.
- Your passion becomes a source of comfort, energy, or inspiration.

Example

After months of painting, Anna held a small exhibit to showcase her work. It wasn't about the accolades but about celebrating her journey and sharing her story through her art.

Reflective Question: How has engaging with a passion, past or present, helped me navigate my emotions and find purpose?

Reawakening your passions isn't just about rediscovering joy—it's about using them as a tool for personal growth. Engaging with something you love teaches you resilience, fosters creativity, and reconnects you with your sense of purpose.

How to Cultivate Passions for Growth

- **Set Goals:** Whether it's completing a project, learning a new skill, or simply dedicating time each week to your passion, setting goals keeps you motivated.
- **Share Your Passion:** Sharing your interests with others—whether through teaching, collaborating, or simply discussing—enhances your connection to them.
- **Reflect on Your Journey:** Keep a journal to track how engaging with your passion impacts your emotions, mindset, and overall well-being.

Reflective Question: How can I use my passion to fuel personal growth and strengthen my sense of self?

Your passions are the seeds of your inner garden, waiting for the right conditions to grow. You create an environment where your passions can flourish by reconnecting with what brings you joy and embracing new experiences.

Anna's journey back to art is a testament to the power of passion as a healing force. Just as she transformed her grief into creativity, you, too, can use your passions to rediscover your inner flame, cultivate personal growth, and create a life filled with meaning and fulfillment.

Remember, your garden may take time to bloom, but every step you take-no matter how small-is a step towards creating something beautiful. Nurture your passions, and watch your life flourish in ways you never imagined.

Chapter 15

Solitude: A Gateway to Strength

Is solitude a source of strength or an abyss of loneliness? This question often arises during heartbreak, when alone time can feel both necessary and overwhelming. Solitude is often misunderstood, its quietness mistaken for emptiness and its stillness for isolation. However, when embraced with the right mindset, solitude can be a powerful tool for self-discovery and rejuvenation.

In this chapter, we'll explore the difference between being alone and feeling lonely, confront common fears about solitude, and uncover its transformative potential. Through practical methods, we'll learn how to harness the power of solitude to create a space for personal growth, reflection, and healing.

Solitude and loneliness are often used interchangeably but fundamentally different experiences.

- **Being Alone:** This is a physical state—a choice to spend time with yourself. It offers freedom, independence, and space for reflection.
- **Feeling Lonely:** This is an emotional state—a sense of disconnection from others, even in their presence. Loneliness stems not from being alone but from feeling unseen or unsupported.

Understanding this distinction is key to reframing solitude as a source of empowerment rather than a cause for despair.

Reflective Question: Do I see alone time as an opportunity or a challenge, and why?

Many people fear solitude because it confronts them with their own thoughts and emotions. Common fears and misconceptions include:

- **Fear of Facing Emotions:** Being alone can bring unresolved feelings to the surface, which might feel overwhelming.
- **Misconception of Isolation:** Solitude is often seen as synonymous with social withdrawal, leading to a sense of exclusion.
- **Societal Pressure:** Choosing solitude might feel countercultural or even selfish in a world that glorifies busyness and connection.

Acknowledging these challenges is the first step towards overcoming them. Solitude isn't about avoiding others—it's about connecting more deeply with yourself.

Reflective Question: What fears or beliefs about solitude might be holding me back from embracing it?

Solitude, when embraced intentionally, can be a transformative experience. It provides:

1. **Time for Introspection:** Without external distractions, you can explore your thoughts, values, and aspirations more deeply.
2. **Clarity and Focus:** Solitude allows you to pause and prioritise, helping you make decisions that align with your true self.
3. **Creative Renewal:** Many artists, writers, and thinkers credit solitude as the birthplace of their greatest ideas.

Think of solitude as a blank canvas—it's a space where you can paint the life you want to create, free from external influences.

Reflective Question: How can I use solitude to reconnect with my authentic self?

Practical Methods for Embracing Solitude

To harness the power of solitude, it's important to approach it intentionally. Here are practical ways to make the most of your alone time:

1. **Set Boundaries:** Communicate your need for alone time to others. Let them know it's not about pushing them away but about prioritising your well-being.
2. **Create a Sacred Space:** Dedicate a physical area for solitude, such as a cosy corner or a spot in nature. Fill it with things that bring you comfort and inspiration.
3. **Practice Mindful Activities:** Engage in activities that encourage presence, like journaling, meditating, or walking. These practices help ground you in the moment.
4. **Set Intentions for Solitude:** Approach your alone time with purpose. Decide what you want to explore or achieve during this period, whether it's reflection, creativity, or relaxation.
5. **Limit Distractions:** Use solitude to unplug from digital devices and external noise.

Embrace the quiet as an opportunity to listen to your inner voice.

Reflective Question: How can I create a sacred space or routine that honours my need for solitude?

Solitude isn't about isolation—it's about empowerment. By reframing alone time as an opportunity rather than a limitation, you can transform it into a practice of self-care and personal growth.

- **From Fear to Freedom:** Instead of fearing your own thoughts, view them as a guide to understanding yourself more deeply.
- **From Absence to Abundance:** Rather than focusing on what's missing, appreciate what you gain from solitude—clarity, peace, and renewal.
- **From Silence to Insight:** Embrace the quiet as a space for creativity and self-discovery.

Reflective Question: How has my perception of solitude shifted, and what opportunities do I now see in being alone?

While solitude offers many benefits, balance is key. Too much time alone can lead to isolation, just as too much social activity can feel overwhelming. Finding the right balance ensures that your solitude nourishes you without disconnecting you from others.

Tips for Finding Balance

- Alternate periods of solitude with moments of connection, whether it's spending time with loved ones or participating in a community activity.
- Use solitude to recharge so that you can engage more fully in your relationships and responsibilities.
- Reflect regularly on how solitude is serving you and make adjustments as needed.

Reflective Question: How can I balance solitude and connection that feels right for me?

When embraced intentionally, solitude is a powerful source of strength. It offers a space to reflect, heal, and grow, enabling you to reconnect with your inner self and align with your values.

Like the quiet of winter that prepares the garden for spring, solitude creates the conditions for renewal. It's not an abyss to fear but a sanctuary to cherish—a reminder that being alone doesn't mean being lonely.

As you continue your journey, let solitude be a tool for empowerment, a gateway to self-discovery, and a foundation for a whole and authentic life. Through solitude, you'll find that your inner flame burns brighter than ever, illuminating the path to a future filled with purpose and possibility.

Chapter 16

Crafting Your Personal Manifesto

In times of uncertainty, having a guiding light can make all the difference. A personal manifesto is more than just a collection of words—it's a declaration of your mission, beliefs, and aspirations. It serves as a compass, pointing you towards clarity and purpose, especially during the tumultuous journey of self-discovery.

In this chapter, we'll explore the transformative power of creating a personal manifesto. By outlining actionable steps and providing practical tips, you'll learn how to craft a manifesto that resonates deeply with your heart and mind. A personal manifesto is a written statement of your core beliefs, values, and intentions. It acts as a roadmap, reminding you of who you are and what you stand for, even when life feels chaotic. Unlike fleeting thoughts or abstract ideas, a manifesto is concrete—it anchors your vision and empowers you to live with purpose.

Why Create a Manifesto?

- **Clarity:** A manifesto organises your thoughts and gives them structure, helping you define what truly matters.
- **Motivation:** Reading your manifesto during difficult times reignites your inner drive and sense of purpose.
- **Empowerment:** It reminds you of your strength and potential, encouraging you to act in alignment with your beliefs.

Reflective Question: What areas of my life would benefit from greater clarity and focus?

Steps to Craft Your Personal Manifesto

Creating a manifesto doesn't require you to be a professional writer or philosopher. All it takes is introspection, intention, and authenticity. Here's how to begin:

1. Define Your Mission

- **Ask yourself:** What is my purpose right now? What do I want to achieve, both personally and in my relationships?
- Write a mission statement that reflects your aspirations. For example: "My mission is to live

with compassion and courage, building a life rooted in love and growth."

2. Identify Your Core Beliefs

- Reflect on your values and what guides your decisions. Are honesty, creativity, or resilience central to who you are?
- List these beliefs in clear, affirming language. For example: "I believe in the power of kindness to transform lives."

3. Articulate Your Intentions

- Outline specific intentions for how you want to live. These might include personal goals, ways you want to treat others, or habits you want to cultivate.
- **Example:** "I intend to prioritise self-care, speak with integrity, and approach challenges as opportunities for growth."

4. Incorporate Inspiring Language

- Use words and phrases that resonate deeply with you. Let your manifesto feel personal and empowering.

5. Write and Refine

- Draft your manifesto, allowing your thoughts to flow naturally. Then, refine it to ensure it's concise and impactful.

- Keep it flexible—your manifesto should grow and evolve as you do.

Reflective Question: What mission, beliefs, and intentions do I want to declare to myself and the world?

Tips and Best Practices

To create a manifesto that truly resonates, consider these tips:

1. **Keep It Authentic:** Write from your heart, not based on what you think others expect.

   Your manifesto is for you.
2. **Make It Accessible:** Keep your manifesto where you can see it regularly, whether it's written in a journal, displayed on your wall, or saved on your phone.
3. **Use Affirmative Language:** Focus on what you want to embrace, not what you want to avoid. Positive phrasing reinforces your intentions.
4. **Review and Reflect:** Revisit your manifesto periodically to ensure it still reflects your goals and values. Adjust it as needed.
5. **Create a Visual Version:** Turn your manifesto into a piece of art, like a vision board or calligraphy piece, to make it even more inspiring.

Reflective Question: How can I ensure my manifesto remains a meaningful and consistent part of my life?

The power of a manifesto lies in its ability to inspire and guide.

Reflective Question: What impact could a personal manifesto have on my ability to overcome challenges and pursue my goals?

Your personal manifesto is a declaration of who you are, what you believe, and the life you want to create. It's a tool for self-reflection, motivation, and growth—a living document that evolves as you do.

By crafting and living by your manifesto, you affirm your commitment to yourself and your journey. It becomes your guiding light, helping you navigate challenges and stay aligned with your values.

Remember, your manifesto doesn't have to be perfect—it must be yours. Use it as a source of strength, inspiration, and clarity as you continue to rediscover your inner flame and build a life filled with purpose and fulfillment.

Chapter 17

Rediscovering Your True Self

In the wake of heartbreak, we often find ourselves standing at a crossroads, unsure of who we are outside the context of our past relationships. This period of self-reflection can feel like looking into a foggy mirror, trying to recognise your own face amid the haze. The advice to "just be yourself" may sound simple, but it often falls short because it assumes we already know who that self is.

Heartbreak offers a unique opportunity to rediscover your true essence, unshaped by others' expectations or the weight of past roles. By embracing deep self-reflection, you can begin the journey of redefining your identity, reconnecting with your authentic self, and moving forward with renewed clarity and confidence.

When relationships end, they often leave behind questions about identity. Who am I without this person? What parts of me were real, and which were shaped by the relationship?

Common Challenges

- **Blurred Self-Image:** Relationships often blur the line between individual identity and shared roles. Over time, your self-image may become intertwined with the expectations or needs of your partner.
- **Uncertainty:** After a breakup, the freedom to redefine yourself can feel overwhelming rather than liberating.
- **Scepticism Towards Self-Reflection:** Some people view self-reflection as indulgent or unnecessary, worrying it may lead to overthinking or self-absorption.

Acknowledging these challenges is the first step towards overcoming them. Self-reflection isn't about dwelling on the past—it's about understanding yourself better to create a more intentional future.

Reflective Question: What aspects of my identity might have been shaped by my past relationships, and how can I reclaim my sense of self?

The advice to "just be yourself" often feels incomplete because it assumes self-awareness. Many of us don't fully know who we are, especially after significant life changes. Heartbreak can amplify this uncertainty, disconnecting us from our true essence.

Why It's Hard to 'Be Yourself'

- We are constantly evolving, and experiences, relationships, and challenges shape our identity.
- External influences, such as societal expectations or family pressures, can cloud our understanding of who we are.
- The person we think we "should" be often overshadows the person we truly are. Instead of trying to "be yourself," focus on rediscovering yourself. This involves peeling back layers of conditioning, reflecting on your values, and embracing your unique qualities.

Reflective Question: Who am I beneath the expectations of others, and how can I honour that version of myself?

Self-reflection is the process of turning inwards to explore your thoughts, feelings, and experiences. It's about asking meaningful questions and listening to the answers with honesty and curiosity.

Key Questions for Self-Rediscovery

1. What makes me feel most alive and fulfilled?
2. What are my core values, and how do they shape my decisions?

3. What qualities do I admire, and what areas do I want to grow in?
4. What limiting beliefs have I carried, and how can I release them?

After her engagement ended, Sapna felt lost and unsure of her identity. Through journaling, she realised how much of her life had been guided by pleasing others. This insight led her to pursue her passion for teaching, a decision that reignited her sense of purpose.

Reflective Question: What insights can I uncover by asking myself deeper questions?

Tools for Self-Reflection

Self-reflection doesn't have to be overwhelming. Using practical tools can make the process approachable and rewarding.

1. Journaling:

- Write freely about your thoughts, emotions, and experiences.
- Use prompts like, "Who am I when I'm happiest?" or "What do I need to feel whole?"

2. Meditation:

- Spend a few minutes each day in quiet contemplation, focusing on your breath and allowing your thoughts to surface without judgment.

- Guided meditations on self-discovery can provide additional structure.

3. Personal Check-Ins:

- At the end of each day, reflect on moments that felt authentic or fulfilling.
  What do they reveal about your true self?

4. Feedback from Trusted Sources:

- Ask close friends or family members what qualities they admire in you.
  Sometimes others see strengths you've overlooked.

Reflective Question: Which self-reflection tool feels most accessible to me, and how can I begin using it today?

Feeling sceptical about focusing on yourself is natural, especially if you've been conditioned to prioritise others. However, self-reflection isn't about vanity—it's about building a stronger connection to yourself so you can show up more authentically in all areas of life.

Why Self-Reflection Isn't Self-Indulgent

- It helps you identify what truly matters, allowing you to live with intention.
- It builds emotional resilience, enabling you to navigate challenges clearly and confidently.

- It enhances your relationships by fostering self-awareness and empathy.

After reflecting on his priorities, James realised his people-pleasing tendencies were draining his energy. By setting boundaries, he became more present and supportive in his relationships, strengthening his connections with others.

Reflective Question: How can I reframe self-reflection as an act of self-care rather than self-indulgence?

Self-reflection is not about creating a new version of yourself—it's about uncovering your version that has always been there. Heartbreak can act as a catalyst for this process, allowing you to rediscover your passions, values, and unique qualities.

Steps to Redefine Your Identity

1. **List Your Strengths:** Identify the qualities and skills that make you unique.
2. **Explore New Interests:** Try activities or hobbies that align with your values or ignite your curiosity.
3. **Create a Personal Mission Statement:** Write a sentence that captures who you are and what you stand for. For example, "I am someone who values creativity, kindness, and growth, and I strive to live with purpose."

Reflective Question: What steps can I take today to rediscover and celebrate my authentic self?

Rediscovering your true self is a journey, not a destination. It requires patience, curiosity, and a willingness to explore both your strengths and vulnerabilities.

As you move forward, remember that your identity is not defined by your past relationships or others' expectations—it is yours to shape and celebrate. Through self-reflection, you can uncover your unique, unfiltered version of yourself and build a life that feels authentic, fulfilling, and entirely yours.

This journey is an act of courage and love—a gift to yourself that will continue to empower you in ways you never imagined. Take the first step, and watch as your true self begins to shine.

Chapter 18

The Strength of Self-Compassion

Are you your own harshest critic? If so, you're not alone. Many of us hold ourselves to impossibly high standards, offering kindness and understanding to others while reserving judgement and criticism for ourselves. But this inner harshness can be a barrier to healing, keeping us stuck in cycles of self-doubt and shame.

Self-compassion, however, offers a different path—one of understanding, kindness, and acceptance. Far from being a sign of weakness, self-compassion is a profound source of strength. It nurtures your inner flame, helping you cultivate resilience, self-love, and the courage to move forward.

In this chapter, we'll explore the transformative

power of self-compassion, dispel common myths about it, and provide actionable steps to integrate it into your daily life.

Self-compassion is the practice of treating yourself with the same kindness, care, and understanding you would offer to a close friend. It involves acknowledging your struggles without judgment and offering support rather than criticism.

The Three Components of Self-Compassion

(as defined by psychologist Kristin Neff)

1. **Self-Kindness:** Being gentle and understanding with yourself, especially in times of failure or difficulty.
2. **Common Humanity:** Recognising that pain and imperfection are part of the shared human experience rather than isolating yourself in your struggles.
3. **Mindfulness:** Observing your thoughts and feelings without becoming overwhelmed or overly critical.

Reflective Question: How do I currently respond to myself during difficult moments, and how might self-compassion change that response?

Self-compassion plays a vital role in the healing process, particularly after heartbreak. It helps dissolve the barriers of self-doubt and fosters a sense of safety and acceptance that is crucial for emotional recovery.

Benefits of Self-Compassion

- **Emotional Resilience:** Self-compassion strengthens your ability to cope with setbacks by reducing feelings of shame and self-blame.
- **Improved Well-Being:** Research shows that self-compassion is linked to greater happiness, optimism, and life satisfaction.
- **Encourages Growth:** Replacing harsh self-criticism with kindness creates an environment where personal growth can thrive.

After a painful breakup, James initially blamed himself for the relationship's failure. Through self-compassion, he learned to acknowledge his mistakes without harsh judgment, allowing him to focus on growth rather than guilt.

Reflective Question: How might self-compassion help me approach my challenges with greater resilience and understanding?

Self-compassion is often misunderstood as self-indulgence, weakness, or an excuse for laziness. Let's address these misconceptions:

- **Myth 1: Self-Compassion Is Selfish**

  Truth: Self-compassion isn't about ignoring others' needs—it's about recognising that you deserve care and kindness.
- **Myth 2: Self-Compassion Leads to Complacency**

Truth: Far from encouraging complacency, self-compassion motivates you to improve because you believe you are worthy of growth.

- **Myth 3: Self-Compassion Is a Sign of Weakness**

  Truth: Extending kindness to yourself requires immense strength, especially in a world that often equates self-criticism with accountability.

Reflective Question: What misconceptions about self-compassion have prevented me from embracing it, and how can I reframe them?

Integrating self-compassion into your daily life doesn't require dramatic changes—it's about small, intentional shifts in how you treat yourself.

Daily Practices

1. **The Self-Compassion Break:**
   - When you're struggling, pause and say:
     1. "This is a moment of suffering." (Mindfulness)
     2. "Suffering is part of being human." (Common humanity)
     3. "May I be kind to myself in this moment." (Self-kindness)
2. **Write a Self-Compassion Letter:**
   - Write to yourself as if you were comforting a dear friend. Acknowledge your pain, offer support, and remind yourself of your worth.

3. **Reframe Negative Self-Talk:**
    - When critical thoughts arise, ask yourself, "Would I say this to a friend?" Replace harsh words with supportive ones.
4. **Practice Small Acts of Kindness:**
    - Treat yourself with care—whether it's taking a walk, enjoying a hobby, or permitting yourself to rest.

Reflective Question: What small action can I take today to practice self-compassion?

When you embrace self-compassion, you create a foundation for resilience and growth. It allows you to:

- **Reconnect with Your Worth:** Self-compassion reminds you that your value isn't tied to perfection—it's inherent.
- **Navigate Challenges with Grace:** Instead of spiralling into self-criticism, you approach difficulties with understanding and strength.
- **Foster Deeper Connections:** By extending kindness to yourself, you develop greater empathy for others, enriching your relationships.

After struggling with feelings of inadequacy, Priya began a daily gratitude practice focused on her own strengths. Over time, she noticed a profound shift in her confidence and ability to handle challenges.

Reflective Question: How has practicing self-compassion changed the way I view myself and my struggles?

Self-compassion is not a one-time act—it's a lifelong practice. Each time you choose kindness over criticism, you strengthen your inner resilience and nurture your capacity for self-love.

Steps to Cultivate Self-Compassion

1. **Set a Daily Intention:** Begin each day with an affirmation, such as, "I will treat myself with kindness and understanding."
2. **Celebrate Progress:** Acknowledge even small steps towards growth or healing. Self-compassion thrives on recognition, not perfection.
3. **Seek Support:** Surround yourself with people who encourage self-compassion, and consider exploring resources like books or therapy for deeper guidance.

Reflective Question: How can I commit to making self-compassion a consistent part of my life?

As you move forward, remember that self-compassion is not about avoiding challenges—it's about facing them with kindness and courage. You create a safe and supportive space for healing, growth, and transformation by nurturing your inner flame.

Your mistakes or your struggles do not define

you—you are defined by your ability to rise, to learn, and to love yourself through it all. Self-compassion isn't just a practice; it's a promise to yourself that you are worthy of care, respect, and endless possibilities.

Embrace this promise, and watch your resilience and self-love grow stronger each day.

Chapter 19

Building Bridges With Core Values

Understanding your core values is like finding the sturdy beams needed to construct a bridge that connects where you are now with where you aspire to be. These values are the foundation that supports your goals, decisions, and growth, ensuring that every step you take feels authentic and purposeful.

In this chapter, we'll explore how to identify your core values, recognise their significance in shaping your aspirations, and align them with your goals. By embracing this alignment, you empower yourself to create a life that reflects your true essence.

Core values are the guiding principles that define what matters most to you. They influence how you make decisions, interact with others, and pursue your dreams. Without clarity on your values, you risk building a life that feels disconnected or unfulfilling.

Core Values as a Foundation

- They provide stability during times of change.
- They help you prioritise what truly matters.
- They foster a sense of alignment between your actions and your beliefs.

Reflective Question: What principles guide my decisions, and how have they shaped my life so far?

To uncover your core values, reflect on moments when you felt truly content or fulfilled. These experiences often reveal the principles that resonate most deeply with you.

Exercise to Identify Core Values

1. Think about a time when you felt proud or accomplished. What were you doing, and why did it matter to you?
2. Reflect on an experience where you felt deeply connected to others. What qualities were present in that connection?
3. Consider moments of personal growth. What values drove you to improve or persevere?

Reflective Question: What moments of contentment or pride reveal my core values? Once you've identified your core values, acknowledge them as the pillars supporting your journey forward. These values are non-negotiable—they define who you are and what you stand for.

Examples of Core Values

- **Courage:** Taking bold steps, even when the outcome is uncertain.
- **Honesty:** Living with integrity and transparency.
- **Kindness:** Treating yourself and others with compassion and respect.
- **Growth:** Striving for continuous learning and improvement.
- **Freedom:** Valuing independence and the ability to make your own choices.

Exercise

Write down your top five core values. Next to each, jot down how they influence your decisions and what role they play in your aspirations.

Reflective Question: Which values feel most essential to who I am, and how do they support my journey?

Pursuing goals feels natural and rewarding when your goals align with your values. This alignment ensures that your aspirations are rooted in authenticity, not external pressures or fleeting desires.

How to Align Goals with Values

1. **Evaluate Your Goals:** Review your current goals. Do they reflect your values, or do external expectations drive them?
2. **Refine Your Aspirations:** Adjust your goals to better align with your principles. For example, if creativity is a core value, prioritise projects that allow you to express it.
3. **Set Value-Based Intentions:** Create goals that directly reflect your values. For instance, if community is important to you, set a goal to volunteer or join a group that fosters connection.

Reflective Question: How can I align my goals with my values to create a more fulfilling path forward?

Decision-making becomes simpler and more empowering when your actions align with your core values. You no longer second-guess your choices because you know they reflect who you are at your core.

Tips for Making Value-Based Choices

- **Pause and Reflect:** Before making a decision, ask yourself, "Does this align with my values?"
- **Use Values as a Compass:** When faced with uncertainty, let your values guide you towards the most authentic choice.
- **Celebrate Small Wins:** Recognise and celebrate

moments when your actions align with your values. These are milestones on your journey.

Reflective Question: How can I use my values as a compass to confidently navigate decisions?

Aligning your life with your core values doesn't just create a sense of purpose—it transforms how you approach challenges, relationships, and opportunities.

Reflective Question: What changes can I make to ensure my life reflects my core values? Living in alignment with your core values isn't always easy, but the rewards are immense.

You'll experience a deeper sense of fulfillment, build stronger connections, and create a life that feels authentically yours.

Benefits of Value-Driven Living

- **Clarity:** You'll better understand what matters most to you.
- **Confidence:** Making decisions based on your values boosts self-trust and assurance.
- **Purpose:** Every action you take feels meaningful and aligned with your aspirations.

Reflective Question: How has aligning with my values enhanced my sense of purpose and fulfillment?

Your core values are the beams that support the

bridge to your aspirations. By reflecting on what truly matters, acknowledging your principles, and aligning your goals with your values, you're creating a pathway to a meaningful, authentic, purposeful, and rewarding life.

Remember, this journey is uniquely yours. Let your values guide you, and trust that each step forward strengthens the bridge you're building—one that will carry you towards the life you're meant to live.

Part V

Stepping into a Renewed Future

Chapter 20

Milestones: Stepping Stones to Fulfillment

Imagine standing on the edge of a river, its far side representing renewal and fulfillment. To cross it, you don't need to leap the entire distance—you just need to step onto the first stone. Each milestone in your journey is one of these stepping stones, bringing you closer to the life you envision.

Milestones are more than tasks; they are promises to you. They mark progress, celebrate growth, and keep your motivation alive. In this chapter, we'll explore how to break down your dreams into achievable goals, create actionable steps, and celebrate every small victory.

Every big dream starts with a clear vision. To make

it achievable, break it down into smaller, manageable goals. This process ensures that what once seemed overwhelming becomes a series of practical steps.

Steps to Break Down Your Vision

1. **Define Your End Goal:** Visualise what success looks like. Be specific—what will you achieve, and how will it feel?
2. **Identify Key Milestones:** Break your vision into stages or milestones. For example, if your goal is to start a business, milestones might include researching your industry, creating a business plan, and launching a pilot project.
3. **Set Priorities:** Determine which milestones are critical and should be tackled first.

Focus on what will create the most impact or momentum.

If your dream is to run a marathon, your milestones might include:

- Choosing a training plan.
- Completing a 5K race.
- Building up to longer distances.

Reflective Question: What milestones will bring me closer to my vision, and which should I focus on first?

Once you've identified your milestones, it's time to create a roadmap for achieving them. This involves breaking each milestone into concrete actions and setting a realistic timeline.

How to Create Actionable Steps

1. **Detail the Actions:** Write down every step needed to achieve each milestone. Be as specific as possible.
    - **Example:** If a milestone is "Complete a business plan," your steps might include researching templates, outlining your goals, and drafting the financial section.
2. **Set Deadlines:** Assign a timeline for each step, ensuring your goals remain measurable and time-bound.
3. **Track Progress:** Use a planner, digital tool, or journal to monitor your progress. Seeing your achievements will keep you motivated.

Reflective Question: What actions can I take today to begin moving toward my next milestone?

Celebrating small victories is essential for maintaining motivation and building momentum. Each accomplishment, no matter how minor, reminds you of your progress and potential.

Ways to Celebrate Small Wins

1. **Acknowledge Your Efforts:** Take a moment to reflect on what you've achieved and the effort it required.

2. **Reward Yourself:** Treat yourself to something meaningful, whether it's a favourite meal, a new book, or a relaxing evening.
3. **Share Your Success:** Share your progress with a trusted friend or mentor who can celebrate with you and offer encouragement.

When Deepali completed her first 5K as part of her marathon training, she treated herself to a new pair of running shoes—a reminder of how far she'd come and a motivator for the next step.

Reflective Question: How can I celebrate my progress in a meaningful and motivating way?

Every journey faces challenges, but setbacks don't have to derail your progress. By anticipating obstacles and planning for them, you can navigate challenges with resilience.

Strategies for Handling Setbacks

1. **Reframe the Challenge:** View setbacks as opportunities to learn and grow rather than as failures.
2. **Adjust Your Plan:** If one approach doesn't work, pivot and try another. Flexibility is key to staying on track.
3. **Lean on Support:** Seek encouragement from friends, mentors, or communities who can offer perspective and motivation.

When Peter's initial business pitch was rejected, he used the feedback to refine his plan. The improved pitch not only secured funding but also strengthened his confidence.

Reflective Question: How can I use setbacks as stepping stones rather than stumbling blocks?

Your milestones aren't just tasks to check off but meaningful markers of your growth and commitment. Treat each one as a promise to yourself, a declaration of your determination and vision.

How to Make Milestones Meaningful

1. **Connect Them to Your Values:** Ensure each milestone aligns with your core principles and long-term aspirations.
2. **Reflect on Their Impact:** Take time to appreciate how each milestone moves you closer to your ultimate goal.
3. **Document the Journey:** Keep a journal or photo log of your milestones. Looking back on your progress will remind you of your strength and perseverance.

Reflective Question: How does achieving this milestone align with my values and vision for the future?

As you cross each stepping stone, you'll notice something powerful: momentum. Every milestone you achieve builds confidence, clarity, and excitement for the next one.

Tips for Building Momentum

- **Focus on One Step at a Time:** Avoid being overwhelmed by concentrating on the milestones directly ahead.
- **Stay Flexible:** Adjust your goals and timeline as needed to reflect your growth and changing circumstances.
- **Celebrate the Journey:** Remember, the journey itself is just as important as the destination.

Reflective Question: How can I maintain momentum while staying present and flexible in my journey?

Each milestone you achieve is a step closer to the life you envision. By breaking down your vision into actionable goals, celebrating small victories, and embracing challenges as opportunities, you're building a bridge to renewal and fulfillment—one stepping stone at a time.

Remember, this journey is uniquely yours. Each milestone is a testament to your courage, resilience, and commitment to growth. With determination and grace, you'll cross the river and step confidently into the life you've always imagined.

Chapter 21

Redefining Success for New Beginnings

What does success mean to you? The word conjures images of achievement, wealth, or recognition for many. But when embarking on new beginnings, success takes on a more personal and transformative meaning. It becomes less about external validation and more about inner fulfillment and growth.

In this chapter, we'll redefine success as a fluid journey, explore how traditional views can limit our potential, and lay the foundation for a more authentic framework. By integrating resilience, adaptability, and passion into your understanding of success, you'll uncover a meaningful path that aligns with your true self.

Traditional definitions of success often view it as a destination—a specific goal to be achieved, like landing a dream job or reaching a milestone. However, this perspective can feel restrictive, especially in the context of personal growth and new beginnings.

Why Success Is a Journey

- Life is ever-changing, and so are your goals and values. Success should evolve with you.
- Viewing success as a journey allows you to celebrate progress and growth, not just results.
- It fosters a sense of purpose and fulfillment, even during challenges or setbacks.

Consider Natasha, who started her own business after years in a corporate job. Initially, she defined success as earning a certain income. Over time, she realised that building meaningful relationships with her clients and pursuing her passion brought her greater fulfillment.

Reflective Question: How can I shift my perspective to see success as a continuous journey rather than a fixed endpoint?

Traditional views of success often prioritise societal expectations—like financial status, career advancement, or external recognition. While these markers can be valuable, they don't always align with personal values or bring lasting satisfaction.

The Limitations of Traditional Success

- It can lead to burnout if driven by external pressures rather than internal motivation.

- It often overlooks intangible achievements, like personal growth or emotional well-being.
- It may discourage risk-taking, as failure is seen as the opposite of success. Redefine success on your terms by focusing on what brings you joy, purpose, and a sense of alignment with your values.

Reflective Question: In what ways have traditional views of success limited me, and how can I redefine success to reflect my true self?

To embrace new beginnings with clarity and purpose, build a framework of success based on resilience, adaptability, and passion.

1. Resilience

Success isn't about avoiding challenges—it's about how you navigate them. Resilience helps you persevere through setbacks and emerge stronger.

- **Practice:** Reflect on past challenges and the strengths you developed as a result. Use these lessons to build confidence in your ability to face future obstacles.

2. Adaptability

Life is full of unexpected changes. Success requires the ability to adapt, pivot, and embrace new opportunities.

- **Practice:** Stay open to new possibilities by

adopting a growth mindset. Ask yourself, "What can I learn from this situation?"

3. Passion

Passion fuels motivation and helps you stay connected to your purpose. When your actions align with your passions, success feels more meaningful.

- **Practice:** Identify activities or goals that ignite your enthusiasm and prioritise them in your daily life.

Reflective Question: How can I incorporate resilience, adaptability, and passion into my personal definition of success?

To redefine success for yourself, reflect on your values, experiences, and aspirations. This process will help you create a vision that feels authentic and inspiring.

Steps to Reimagine Success

1. **Reflect on Past Achievements:** Identify moments when you felt truly successful. What made those experiences meaningful?
2. **Define Fulfillment:** Write down what fulfillment looks like for you. Is it about relationships, creativity, impact, or something else?
3. **Set Aligned Goals:** Create goals that reflect your redefined vision of success.

Ensure they prioritise growth and authenticity over external validation.

After a significant life transition, Rohan realised his fulfillment came from mentoring others. He shifted his career focus to education, finding success in the joy of helping students grow.

Reflective Question: What steps can I take today to align my goals with my redefined vision of success?

With a redefined understanding of success, new beginnings become opportunities for exploration and growth rather than daunting challenges. By staying true to your values and focusing on your journey, you create a foundation for lasting fulfillment.

Tips for Embracing New Beginnings

- **Start Small:** Break down your aspirations into manageable steps, celebrating each milestone along the way.
- **Stay Open:** Allow your definition of success to evolve as you grow and encounter new experiences.
- **Celebrate Progress:** Recognise and honour your efforts, regardless of the outcome.

  Every step forward is a success.

Reflective Question: How can I approach my next beginning with a renewed sense of purpose and authenticity?

True success isn't about meeting a universal standard but embracing your unique journey. By redefining success as a fluid, evolving process rooted in personal growth and fulfillment, you empower yourself to pursue a meaningful life that aligns with your values.

Every milestone, every challenge, and every new beginning becomes an opportunity to grow, adapt, and thrive. As you continue your journey, remember that success is not measured by where you end up but by how fully and authentically you live.

Let this new definition of success inspire you to take bold steps forward, celebrating each moment as a testament to your strength, passion, and resilience.

Chapter 22

Rising From the Ashes: Lessons from the Phoenix

The phoenix, a mythical bird that rises anew from its ashes, has long been a symbol of rebirth and renewal. Its story resonates because it mirrors the human experience: even in our darkest moments, we have the potential to rise, stronger and more radiant than before.

In this chapter, we'll explore inspiring stories of individuals who, like the phoenix, faced profound setbacks yet emerged transformed. By examining the challenges they endured and the strategies they employed, we'll uncover the power of resilience and its role in turning adversity into triumph. These stories will remind you that no matter how heavy the weight of heartbreak or hardship, you have the strength to soar to new heights.

Before diving into the stories, consider why the phoenix remains a powerful metaphor. The bird doesn't simply endure destruction—it embraces it as a necessary step in its renewal cycle. Similarly, life's challenges, while painful, can serve as catalysts for profound transformation when met with courage and intention.

The Phoenix Mindset

- **Acceptance:** Acknowledging the difficulty without letting it define your future.
- **Growth:** Seeing challenges as opportunities to rebuild stronger.
- **Resilience:** Continuing forward despite setbacks, trusting in your ability to overcome.

Reflective Question: How can I begin to view my struggles as an integral part of my journey towards renewal?

Case Study: From Setback to Triumph

Radhika's Story: Rising After Loss

Radhika was a successful entrepreneur who lost everything—her business, home, and sense of purpose—after a series of unforeseen financial setbacks. For months, she felt defeated, consumed by feelings of failure and self-doubt.

The Turning Point

One day, Radhika read about the concept of post-traumatic growth, which highlights the possibility of thriving after adversity. Inspired, she began to reframe her loss as an opportunity to start anew.

Strategies Radhika Used

1. **Mindset Shift:** Radhika stopped seeing her loss as the end and began viewing it as a blank slate. She asked herself, "What can I create from here?"
2. **Leaning on Community:** She contacted mentors and friends who offered guidance and support, reminding her she wasn't alone.
3. **Setting Incremental Goals:** Instead of rebuilding everything at once, Radhika focused on small, achievable milestones, like developing a new business idea and saving for a fresh start.

Outcome

Radhika launched a new venture aligned with her core values, combining her skills with a deeper sense of purpose. Today, she credits her past setbacks as the foundation for her most meaningful successes.

Reflective Question: What small steps can I take today to begin rising from my own challenges?

Radhika's story illustrates resilience in action—the ability to adapt, recover, and grow stronger in the face of adversity. Resilience is not a trait you're born with; it's a skill you can cultivate through intentional practice.

Key Elements of Resilience

1. **Emotional Regulation:** Learning to manage emotions so they don't overwhelm you during difficult times.
2. **Optimism:** Cultivating a belief in your ability to navigate challenges and create a brighter future.
3. **Problem-Solving Skills:** Breaking down obstacles into manageable steps and seeking creative solutions.
4. **Support Networks:** Surround yourself with people who uplift and encourage you. Research has shown that people who practice gratitude and mindfulness are better equipped to bounce back from setbacks, as these practices enhance emotional resilience and perspective.

Reflective Question: How can I incorporate resilience-building practices into my daily life?

Studies on resilience and recovery highlight the universal nature of overcoming adversity:

- **Post-Traumatic Growth:** Research indicates that many individuals report increased personal strength, deeper relationships, and a greater appreciation for life after experiencing significant challenges.

- **Neuroplasticity:** The brain's ability to adapt and rewire itself supports the idea that we can develop new thought patterns and behaviours to navigate hardship effectively.
- **Social Connection:** Multiple studies have shown that strong social ties are critical in overcoming adversity and achieving personal growth.

Reflective Question: How can I leverage these insights to support my journey towards renewal?

Inspiration From Shared Stories

Here are additional examples of individuals who turned heartbreak into triumph:

1. **Carlos's Career Reinvention:** After being laid off from his dream job, Carlos used the time to reevaluate his passions. He retrained in a new field and now works in a role that brings him fulfillment and balance.
2. **Swati's Emotional Growth:** After a painful divorce, Swati began journaling daily to process her feelings. Over time, she found clarity about what she wanted from life and built stronger, healthier relationships.
3. **Andrew's Health Transformation:** A health scare motivated Andrew to embrace a lifestyle centered on wellness. He became an advocate for others facing similar challenges, finding purpose in helping others heal.

Reflective Question: What lessons can I draw from others' stories to inspire my journey?

The phoenix doesn't rise from its ashes by chance—it transforms through intention, effort, and resilience. Similarly, your journey towards renewal requires embracing your challenges as opportunities for growth and channeling your strength to create a brighter future.

Actionable Steps for Rising from Adversity

1. **Reframe Your Perspective:** Instead of asking, "Why did this happen to me?" ask, "What can I learn from this?"
2. **Set a Vision for Renewal:** Define what "rising anew" looks like for you. What would fulfillment feel like?
3. **Take One Step at a Time:** Focus on progress, not perfection. Every small victory brings you closer to your goal.
4. **Celebrate Your Growth:** Acknowledge how far you've come, even if the journey ahead feels long.

Reflective Question: How can I channel my inner phoenix to rise from my challenges?

The stories of those who have risen from profound setbacks remind us of a powerful truth:

No matter how low we feel, there is always the

potential to rise. With resilience, intention, and the support of others, you too can transform your struggles into stepping stones towards a stronger, more radiant version of yourself.

Let the image of the phoenix inspire you as you continue your journey. Remember, the ashes of heartbreak are not the end—they are the beginning of your ascent to new heights. Trust in your ability to soar.

Chapter 23

Crafting Your Roadmap to a Vibrant New Beginning

Embarking on a journey towards a vibrant new beginning can feel overwhelming, but with a clear and methodical plan, the path becomes manageable and empowering. A personal roadmap serves as your guide—a step-by-step plan that aligns with your aspirations and helps you confidently navigate uncertainties.

This chapter will provide the tools to create a roadmap that resonates with your inner desires, equips you with essential resources, and helps you avoid common pitfalls. This plan gives you a powerful tool to steer your life towards a future filled with promise and potential.

Step 1: Set Clear, Achievable Goals

The first step in creating your roadmap is identifying your destination. These goals should reflect your deepest aspirations and be both meaningful and realistic.

How to Set Effective Goals

1. **Be Specific:** Instead of setting vague goals like "be happier," aim for something tangible, such as "spend 30 minutes each day on an activity that brings me joy."
2. **Ensure They Resonate:** Your goals should align with your core values and passions.

   If they don't excite or inspire you, revisit them.
3. **Break Them Down:** Divide larger goals into smaller, actionable steps. For example, if your goal is to learn a new skill, your steps might include researching courses, enrolling in one, and dedicating time weekly to practice.

Reflective Question: What goals truly resonate with my desires and values, and how can I break them into achievable steps?

Step 2: Identify Resources and Support Systems

Every journey requires tools and allies. Identifying the resources and support systems you need will make your roadmap more actionable and ensure you're prepared for challenges.

How to Identify Resources

- **Knowledge:** What do you need to learn to achieve your goals? Books, online courses, or mentors can be valuable resources.
- **People:** Surround yourself with supportive individuals who encourage your growth.

  This could include friends, family, mentors, or support groups.
- **Practical Tools:** Identify tangible resources like apps, planners, or financial means that can aid your progress.

If you want to start a business, resources might include a business mentor, online entrepreneurship courses, and a budgeting app to track expenses.

Reflective Question: What resources and support systems can I rely on to help me navigate this journey?

Step 3: Design a Step-by-Step Roadmap

Your roadmap should be a clear, actionable guide that takes you from where you are now to where you want to be. Each step should act as a beacon, illuminating the path ahead.

How to Create Your Roadmap

1. **List Your Steps:** Write down every action you need to take to reach your goal, in order of priority.
2. **Set Timelines:** Assign realistic deadlines to

each step, ensuring you stay on track without overwhelming yourself.

3. **Build Flexibility:** Allow room for adjustments. Life is unpredictable, and your roadmap should adapt as needed.

If your goal is to improve physical health, your roadmap might include:

- Researching fitness routines (Week 1).
- Joining a gym or starting a home workout plan (Week 2).
- Scheduling workouts three times a week (Week 3).

Reflective Question: What specific steps and timelines will guide me towards my goal?

Step 4: Avoid Common Pitfalls

Even with a solid plan, it's easy to encounter roadblocks. Being aware of common pitfalls and how to overcome them can keep you moving forward.

Common Pitfalls and How to Avoid Them

- **Overloading Your Schedule:** Break tasks into manageable chunks and prioritise self-care.
- **Fear of Failure:** Embrace setbacks as opportunities to learn and grow. Failure is a natural part of progress.

- **Losing Motivation:** Regularly revisit your "why"—why this goal matters to you—and celebrate small victories to stay inspired.

Reflective Question: How can I anticipate and prepare for potential challenges?

Step 5: Measure Progress and Adjust Your Course

A successful roadmap isn't static; it evolves with you. Measuring your progress and making adjustments ensures you stay aligned with your goals and values.

How to Track and Adjust Your Progress

- **Review Regularly:** Set aside time weekly or monthly to assess your progress.

  What's working? What needs to change?
- **Celebrate Wins:** Recognise and reward yourself for every milestone, no matter how small.
- **Stay Flexible:** If your goals or circumstances change, update your roadmap to reflect your new direction.

Vanshika set a goal to write a book but found her initial timeline too ambitious. She reassessed her roadmap and adjusted her schedule to write fewer pages per week, making her goal more sustainable.

Reflective Question: How can I regularly assess and refine my roadmap to align with my aspirations?

Your roadmap is more than a plan—it's a declaration of your commitment to growth and renewal. It guides you through uncertainties and reminds you that each step is progress towards a brighter future, no matter how small.

By setting clear goals, identifying resources, designing actionable steps, avoiding pitfalls, and adjusting as needed, you empower yourself to embrace new beginnings with confidence and purpose.

Remember, this journey is uniquely yours. Trust in your roadmap, and take each step with determination and grace. Your vibrant new beginning is closer than you think.

Chapter 24

The Dance Between Change and Stability

Life's journey often feels like a delicate dance between change and stability—two forces that may seem at odds but, when balanced, create harmony and growth. Change brings opportunities and fresh perspectives, while stability offers the grounding needed to sustain that growth. Together, they allow us to embrace new beginnings with both confidence and curiosity.

In this chapter, we'll explore how change and stability coexist, drawing on real-world examples and personal stories to illustrate their dynamics. You'll gain insights into maintaining a stable foundation while embracing the exhilarating winds of change, crafting a secure yet adventurous life.

Change is the spark that ignites transformation. It invites you to step outside your comfort zone, explore new possibilities, and grow in unexpected ways. Without change, life can feel stagnant—but with it, comes the potential for discovery and renewal.

Why Change Matters

- It introduces fresh perspectives, helping you see the world—and yourself—in new ways.
- It fosters adaptability, teaching you to navigate life's unpredictability with resilience.
- It propels growth, encouraging you to challenge limits and embrace possibilities.

After losing her job, Aditi saw change as an opportunity to pivot towards a career aligned with her passions. This shift reignited her enthusiasm and opened doors she never imagined.

Reflective Question: How has change in my life led to growth or unexpected opportunities?

While change fuels growth, stability provides the solid ground from which you can leap. It's the steady rhythm in life's dance, offering a sense of security and consistency that keeps you grounded during times of uncertainty.

Why Stability Matters

- It nurtures a sense of safety, allowing you to take risks without fear of losing your footing.

- It creates routines and habits that support long-term well-being and productivity.
- It reinforces your core values and beliefs, acting as a compass when navigating change.

Joseph embraced change by moving to a new city but found stability by maintaining his morning routine of meditation and exercise. This grounding practice gave him the confidence to adapt to his new environment.

Reflective Question: What aspects of my life provide stability, and how can I strengthen them?

The key to a fulfilling life is not choosing one over the other but learning to balance change and stability. This balance enables you to move forward with a sense of adventure while staying true to your roots.

How to Harmonise Change and Stability

1. **Establish Anchors:** Identify the constants in your life—relationships, values, or routines—that provide a sense of stability.
2. **Welcome Change Gradually:** Introduce change in small, manageable steps to ensure it feels exciting rather than overwhelming.
3. **Adapt Your Mindset:** View change and stability as complementary forces, each enriching your life in different ways.

Nisha wanted to explore new hobbies but felt uneasy about disrupting her schedule. She embraced change while maintaining her established routines by setting aside one evening a week for creative pursuits.

Reflective Question: What steps can I take to create a balance between change and stability in my life?

Real-Life Scenarios

Balancing change and stability plays out differently in various life situations. Here are a few examples:

1. **Career Transitions:**
   - **Change:** Starting a new job or shifting industries.
   - **Stability:** Maintaining professional networks and using transferable skills to ease the transition.
2. **Moving to a New Place:**
   - **Change:** Adapting to a new environment and meeting new people.
   - **Stability:** Bringing familiar routines and cherished belongings to create a sense of home.
3. **Personal Growth:**
   - **Change:** Exploring new hobbies or perspectives.
   - **Stability:** Ground yourself in your core values and maintain close relationships.

Reflective Question: How can I apply these principles to balance change and stability in my own life transitions?

Reflective Question: What lessons from others' experiences can I apply to my own dance between change and stability?

Successfully balancing change and stability isn't about perfection but intentionality. By creating a foundation of stability, you give yourself the freedom to embrace change without fear. And by welcoming change, you ensure your life remains dynamic and full of possibility.

Tips for Crafting Balance

- **Stay Curious:** Embrace a mindset of exploration, viewing change as an opportunity rather than a threat.
- **Ground Yourself:** Strengthen your anchors, such as close relationships or daily rituals, to provide consistency.
- **Celebrate Both:** Acknowledge the growth brought by change and the comfort of stability.

Reflective Question: How can I intentionally weave both stability and change into the fabric of my life?

The interplay of change and stability is unique to each person. By learning to harmonise these forces, you can create a life that feels both secure and adventurous—a life that reflects your values while embracing new possibilities.

Remember, the dance between change and stability is not a choice between opposites but a rhythm to master. With every step, you're shaping a future that is as dynamic as it is grounded, as exciting as it is secure. Embrace the dance, and let it lead you to a life of fulfillment and joy.

Chapter 25

Embracing Courage to Step into New Beginnings

What does it take to summon the courage to step boldly into a new beginning? The answer lies in understanding the intricate relationship between fear and bravery. Fear, often viewed as an obstacle, is not the villain—the shadow defines the light of courage. Without fear, there can be no bravery, for courage is born when we choose to act despite our doubts and uncertainties.

This final chapter is an invitation to reframe your perspective on fear and embrace the courage within you. You'll uncover the tools to step into a new beginning with confidence and purpose through stories of transformation, actionable strategies, and empowering insights.

Fear is a natural response to the unknown. It tightens its grip when we're faced with uncertainty, whispering all the reasons we should stay where we are. But fear also has a purpose—it highlights what matters most and challenges us to rise above it.

The Role of Fear

- **Signals Growth:** Fear often appears when we're on the brink of change, indicating an opportunity to grow.
- **Defines Courage:** Courage isn't the absence of fear; it's the decision to move forward in spite of it.
- **Fuels Awareness:** Fear forces us to pause and reflect, allowing us to assess risks and prepare for what lies ahead.

Fear loomed large when Ronit decided to move to a new country for a fresh start. He worried about leaving his comfort zone, but he realised that his fear pointed to the significance of this step in his journey.

Reflective Question: How has fear shown up in my life, and how can I view it as an ally rather than an adversary?

Reflective Question: What small step can I take today to begin shifting my fear into courage?

Fear doesn't have to paralyse you. With the right strategies, you can use it as a catalyst for action and growth.

Steps to Reframe Fear

1. **Acknowledge It:** Instead of avoiding or suppressing fear, name it. Acknowledging your fear reduces its power over you.
2. **Break It Down:** Identify what specifically you're afraid of. Often, fears are based on uncertainties that can be addressed with preparation.
3. **Take Small Steps:** Courage builds with action. Start small—each step forward weakens fear's grip and strengthens your confidence.
4. **Visualise Success:** Imagine yourself overcoming the fear and succeeding. This mental rehearsal helps shift your focus from doubt to infinite possibilities.
5. **Lean on Support:** Share your fears with trusted friends or mentors. Their perspective and encouragement can provide the boost you need.

Reflective Question: How can I use fear as a guide to identify areas where I need to grow?

Courage isn't a trait you're born with—it's a skill you can develop through intentional practice.

Practices to Cultivate Courage

1. **Build Resilience:** Strengthen your ability to bounce back from setbacks by reflecting on past challenges you've overcome.
2. **Celebrate Progress:** Recognise and celebrate

every act of bravery, no matter how small. Each victory reinforces your courage.

3. **Adopt a Growth Mindset:** Embrace the belief that every experience, even failure, contributes to your growth and learning.
4. **Create a Mantra:** Develop a phrase to remind yourself of your strength. For example, "I am capable of handling whatever comes my way."
5. **Practice Self-Compassion:** Treat yourself with kindness when fear arises. Acknowledging your humanity helps you move forward without judgment.

Reflective Question: What practices can I incorporate to strengthen my courage?

A new beginning is both an ending and a starting point. It's natural to feel a mix of fear and excitement as you prepare to step forward. But remember: the courage to embrace change doesn't come from eliminating fear—it comes from choosing to act despite it.

How to Embrace Your New Beginning

- **Set an Intention:** Define what you want this new chapter to represent. Is it about growth, discovery, healing, or something else?
- **Trust the Process:** Progress isn't always linear. Be patient with yourself as you navigate the twists and turns of your journey.

- **Stay Open:** Approach your new beginning with curiosity, embracing the opportunities and lessons it brings.

Reflective Question: What intention can I set to guide me as I step into this new beginning?

As we conclude this journey together, remember that you can rise from the ashes of heartbreak with grace and strength. Fear may accompany you, but it doesn't define you. No matter how small, each act of courage propels you closer to a life filled with purpose, joy, and fulfillment.

Embrace the dance between fear and bravery. Use your newfound insights, the stories shared, and the strategies you've learned to guide you. The courage you need is already within you—it's been there all along, waiting for you to uncover it.

Step boldly into your new beginning. This is your time to soar.